We Should Soon Become Respectable

TL &H | TRUTHS, LIES, AND HISTORIES OF NASHVILLE

TRUTHS, LIES, AND HISTORIES OF NASHVILLE
Betsy T. Phillips, *series editor*

As a lead-up to Nashville's 250th anniversary in 2029, Vanderbilt University Press is publishing an ambitious new series consisting of 25 small volumes designed to bridge the gap between what scholars and experts know about the city and what the public thinks it knows.

These are the stories that have never been told, the truths behind the oft-told tales, the things that keep us in love with the city, and the parts of the past that have broken our hearts, with a priority on traditionally underrepresented perspectives and untold stories.

WE SHOULD SOON BECOME RESPECTABLE

NASHVILLE'S OWN

TIMOTHY DEMONBREUN

BY

ELIZABETH ELKINS

TRUTH, LIES, *and* HISTORIES *of* NASHVILLE
VOLUME II

VANDERBILT UNIVERSITY PRESS
Nashville, Tennessee

First printing 2022

LIBRARY OF CONGRESS CATALOGING-IN-PUBLICATION DATA

Names: Elkins, Elizabeth, 1974– author.
Title: We should soon become respectable : Nashville's own Timothy Demonbreun / Elizabeth Elkins.
Other titles: Truths, lies, and histories of Nashville ; v. 2.
Description: Nashville, Tennessee : Vanderbilt University Press, [2022] | Series: Truths, lies, and histories of Nashville ; volume II | Includes bibliographical references.
Identifiers: LCCN 2021043216 (print) | LCCN 2021043217 (ebook) | ISBN 9780826504487 (paperback) | ISBN 9780826504494 (epub) | ISBN 9780826504500 (pdf)
Subjects: LCSH: De Monbreun, Jacques Timothe Boucher, sieur, 1747–1826. | Fur traders—Tennessee—Nashville—Biography. | Nashville (Tenn.)—Biography.
Classification: LCC F444.N253 D44 2022 (print) | LCC F444.N253 (ebook) | DDC 976.8/55—dc23

LC record available at https://lccn.loc.gov/2021043216
LC ebook record available at https://lccn.loc.gov/2021043217

To Nashville, who no longer uses caves to hide its secrets.

CONTENTS

1

Little Marrowbone

In late October, the hills and hollows where Tennessee's Davidson and Cheatham counties meet feel more like deep Appalachia than suburban Nashville. Just a fifteen-minute drive from the heart of Music City's honkytonks and bachelorette glitz and glamour, Cheatham County is a narrow ice-cream-cone-shaped piece of land where the city ends and the country begins. The leaves on the oaks and hickory trees are deep umber and sticky red, and each passing mile replaces mid-century homes with small farmhouses. If you drive out Eaton Creek Road, you'll keep both hands on the wheel to manage the tricky curves and to dodge the whitetail deer, groundhogs, and occasional bear that might share the asphalt.

The northeast corner of the county is still a remote place. Nashville grabbed the neighboring land to create Beaman Park, but just on the edge of the park's steep terrain is a different world. It's a world of wood-frame houses hidden in the sassafras, where Baptists and Church of Christ parishioners still swap churches on Sunday—and where one of every five or six trailers proudly displays an American flag beside the Stars and Bars. You can smell the honesty, ferocity, love—and a touch of meth—in the air. It's a beautiful and strange land. There are a few weak boundaries: White's Creek Pike and Abernathy Road, the Ashland City Walmart, Blue Springs Road—but at the center of it all is the whispering, shallow creek known as Little Marrowbone.

Just up the hill from the creek is the Demonbreun-Carney cemetery. It used to be attached to the church below, but today it stands on its own, the older, crumbling stones gathered at its highest point, some decorated with off-season splashes of neon yellow and blue flowers. There's a name that repeats from stone to stone, each spelling slightly modified. A name that trips the tongue. A name that challenges the English Scots-Irish bloodlines that soak Middle Tennessee. De Mont Breun. Demumbrine. Demumbra. Demonbreun. One headstone reads:

Jacques Timothe Boucher Sieur de Montbreun

1747–1826

FIGURE 1. The entrance to Demonbreun Cemetery in Cheatham County, also known as Carney or Little Marrowbone Cemetery. Photo by author.

It's shaped mostly like a fleur-de-lis. Someone placed a wreath of plastic flowers on it months, or years, ago.

French Canadian Fur Trader of French Lick
Officer of the American Revolution

FIGURES 2A AND 2B. Timothy is definitely not buried here, in the Demonbreun Cemetery near Little Marrowbone Creek. Photo by author.

Governor in Command of the Illinois Country
Early Resident and Merchant of Nashville
Et Quoy Plus[1]

But Timothé's (let's Anglicize to Timothy moving forward) body is not six feet beneath this stone.

1. "And what more."

FRENCH CANADIAN FUR
TRADER OF FRENCH LICK
OFFICER OF THE
AMERICAN REVOLUTION
GOVERNOR IN COMMAND OF
THE ILLINOIS COUNTRY
EARLY RESIDENT AND
MERCHANT OF NASHVILLE

The tiny town of Joelton is a five-mile drive from the cemetery. It's on the north side of the Devil's Elbow, a treacherous hairpin turn haunted by the ghosts of motorcycle wrecks and teenage dares (plus the victims of one particularly gruesome axe-wielding murderer, an unsolved case which is another book in itself). If you navigate the Devil's Elbow successfully, you've summited Paradise Ridge. Today it's downtown Joelton: Hilltop Pawn-N-Loan, Love-a-Lot Childcare, three churches, and the middle and elementary schools are all in immediate view. But at the south end of town is a curious building: Anderson & Garrett Funeral Home.

The windows don't quite add up, a few distorted with centuries-old glass. The additions are skewed. The front yard seems like it holds the clues to the mystery, outlines of a foundation, perhaps. The swells in the land are off-putting and out of time, they feel man- (or woman-)made. This may have once been the site of Granny Rat's Tavern, reputed house of prostitution, home of great drinks for weary travelers and owned by one tough-as-nails woman of unknown origin, who, most myths and facts agree, loved Timothy. Her name was Elizabeth. They had a lot of children together.

She, on the other hand, is back at Demonbreun Cemetery.

[Obscured by plastic flowers] . . . do not deface the
original tombstone it reads Sacred to the Memory of
Elizabeth Durard
July 24, 1740–Feb 7, 1856
By her son J. B. DeMumbra

The tombstone above it, weathered and lichen-covered, legibly reads "1746–1826."

This Elizabeth, you see, might have been 116 years old when she died. Or 80.

Historical record tells us clearly that she wasn't Timothy's wife. But she certainly had his children—J. D. Demumbra being one of them. And her body, unlike Timothy's, is definitely in the ground here by Little Marrowbone.

It's easy to assume she and Timothy, who were both living in the new town of Fort Nashborough, may have come out here together to hunt and trap fur. It was a doable day trip. The natives (mostly Shawnee) had largely been pushed farther

FIGURE 3. Elizabeth's final resting place at Demonbreun Cemetery. Photo by author.

and farther away. It was a land of vice where their affair was likely celebrated or ignored. The pair knew these hollows. But how she ended up here and he ended up most likely buried under what is now a parking lot in Nashville is a gorgeous and arguably epic tale that involves the French, the English, the Spanish, five or six native tribes, a cave, bullet making, the ever-revolving ownership of land grants—plus, as if that were not enough, a possibly murdered other woman named Therese . . . and a why-don't-you-marry-my-best-friend plot twist regarding another Frenchman named Joseph Derrat.

The challenge in Timothy's story is unravelling the truth from the pretty awesome lies (or misinterpretations), many of which have become a part of Nashville's lore.

We know that most of Elizabeth's and Timothy's "bastard" offspring still live out here in Cheatham County, on the banks and swells of Little Marrowbone. And they've certainly kept the myth alive. They've accepted they're on the wrong side of the legal marriage, though they made excuse after excuse for him in early generations. They've embraced not only their forefather's adultery and uncommon Catholicism, but leaned into his potential manipulative spying and his undeniably important part in creating the city of Nashville. They've fed the fable of the great adventurer until it's bursting at the seams with heroism and manifest destiny.

But when Jacques Timothé Boucher Sieur de Montbreun, known today as Timothy Demonbreun, left French Canada in 1768, it's hard to imagine he had any idea what lay before him. This man with "spindly but strong legs, wide shoulders, steel-blue piercing eyes, prominent cheekbones, thin lips and square set jaw . . . and a prominent nose" (on a lighter note, his descendants allegedly used the strong legs they inherited to lift and move a Volkswagen Beetle blocking the view for photographers when his statue was unveiled in downtown Nashville) can be seen as a picture-perfect frontiersman, a

Davy Crockett–style figure with rivers instead of gaps as his roads. He's a statesman of sorts with a Quebecois accent and a joie de vivre that led him from a rich family near Montreal to a cave on the Cumberland River. His mystery is magnified by his life in that cave and the numerous women he charmed.

When, in 1825, the visiting Marquis de Lafayette toasted Timothy as "the grand old man of Tennessee and first white man to settle the Cumberland country," he was wrong in many ways. By then, Timothy was kicked back in a nice house downtown and he (or fate) had solved all those lady problems. He might have been thinking about how to divide up all the land he was given by the American government for his military service. He might have wondered what could have been if the English had never showed up, if the Spanish had taken the town on the bluffs, if his wife had never been killed, or if he had just headed to New Orleans like most of his cousins . . .

2

The Road to Music Row

If you've ever visited Music Row in Nashville, you've taken the Demonbreun Street exit off of Interstate 40, driven up Demonbreun Street to Demonbreun Hill, and circled around the strange naked dancers (known as *Musica*) before you turned down Seventeenth Avenue to explore the alleys and houses that made country music famous.

But not yet.

FIGURE 4. Demonbreun Hill marks the entrance to Music Row, and, circa 2021, is an increasingly popular nightlife spot. Photo by author.

By the late 1600s, much of the area around the Cumberland River in what is now Tennessee was a hunting ground for Native American tribes including the Creek, Cherokee, Chickasaw, Choctaw, and Shawnee. The river was called Wasioto. Though there were numerous native mounds in the vicinity (and thousands of even-earlier-provenance box grave sites), those Mississippian mound builders and their predecessors had long disappeared. The current tribes were drawn to the area due to the numerous salt licks in the area, which brought game. The abundance of buffalo, deer, and other animals brought French fur traders down from the Illinois Country as early as the late 1600s. They traded primarily with the Shawnee.

Martin Chartier was the first to establish a trading post in the vicinity, likely around 1695. He too was from Quebec, and had made a name for himself exploring the Illinois Country with big names like La Salle and Louis Jolliet, and helping to build two forts, Fort Miami and Fort Crèvecœur. Interestingly enough, he decided to set up this Wasioto post on top of a Mississippian mound, which has since been destroyed but was located between the current site of the Tennessee State Library and Archives and the greenway in the Germantown neighborhood. Chartier was just borrowing the idea from the Shawnee, though, as the tribe had had a post on top of the same mound for many years. He also married a Shawnee woman, which theoretically could be the source of the Timothy-married-a-native-woman theories, as people tended to mix up their "first French fur trader" identities. At least that's the most supported theory in the race of what-European-man-was-in-Nashville first.

As more and more French arrived, the natives began to realize how valuable the area was to traders, and additional tribes began to compete with the Shawnee for the trade. Chartier's post was a casualty of this competition. The French and Indian War brought things to a proverbial head. The land got a new nickname, "the dark and bloody ground," because of numerous hostile attacks. That same war, however, led Timothy out of Quebec to trap game. In 1766, after jaunts all around the Illinois Territory, he discovered a salt lick just north of what would become downtown Nashville. It soon was called French Lick. By then, the French affectionately called the river the "Rivière des Chaouanons," or "River of the Shawnee." Timothy would later establish his trading post on the Shawnee-Chartier mound ("seventy yards off the river, seventy yards off French Lick Creek").

Meanwhile, the British had a similar idea. Led by Virginian Thomas Walker and his Loyal Land Company, an expedition of surveyors and men known as long hunters crossed the Appalachian Mountains. Though they did not come to Nashville, they mapped much of the area and renamed the plateau, gap, and river for Prince William, Duke of Cumberland. Folks like Daniel Boone helped spread the word about the region's unlimited game and great soil for growing. The Cumberland and Ohio River valleys were now officially open for East Coast business.

This soon-to-be-the-state-of-Tennessee land was long at the heart of a set of complex relationships between European powers, between native tribes, and between Europeans and natives. Though one often hears the English settlement story, the area was the setting for countless other complicated political narratives prior. The Spanish and French jockeyed for favor and safety and access to the game and the land. As the British Empire expanded from the east, the land became even more important. Meanwhile, as Americans moved closer to independence, their goals shifted from a focus on the English, and varying alliances between tribes and other European countries multiplied across this western edge of a future-autonomous America. It was, for many decades, essentially the front squall line in the quest for the country: small skirmishes, backdoor alliances, and political wheelings and dealings among these competing powers would determine the current shapes and boundaries of North America.

Timothy, though certainly not the first of the French Canadians to arrive, had a mere two to three years before men from Virginia and the Carolinas began to arrive, eager to stake their claim to the rich land.

However, if you trust the *Memphis Public Ledger* from 1879, you might believe Timothy (they call him Limothe, amazingly) was the very first white man to set foot on the land that would become Nashville:

> [Limothe] organized a party of about 20 men, and, embarking on the Ohio River, in a fleet of pirogues, he set out for the wilderness, seeking a mart for his goods. When he had reached the mouth of what was then called the Shananau, or Cumberland River, they turned their prows up that stream and rowed into a terra incognita, for no white man had ever passed up its dark and turbid waters. Day after day passed and still they paddled on or pushed their frail boats upstream. One day they all, tired and worn out, were slowly driving against the current when they saw before them a huge bluff rising up from the water's edge, crowned with a huge tuft of cedars. Below the bluff appeared a good landing, and, while consulting as to the best point to land, they detected the smell of sulphur. As soon as they landed, while some were making preparations for the evening meal, others followed the "branch" to find the spring whence the sulphur water came. They did not have far to go before they came to the famous "French Lick." To their astonishment they found the surface trod with innumerable tracks, beating down all undergrowth for many yards around. While they were debating these

> wonderful "signs," forth from the cane that surrounded the space flashed a shower of arrows which, however, fell harmless around them. One of them, well acquainted with Indian habits immediately fired his gun into the air, which informed the savages they were friendly. At this indication of peace the Indians showed themselves, but at a safe distance. Though the Frenchmen had no knowledge of these Indians, yet they had sufficient knowledge of the dialect to make known they were friends and allies. The red men had heard of the friendly Frenchmen, and, in fact, some of them had received pay from the wily Gaul. So soon as friendly relations were established, the exploring party made known their intentions and invited the Indians to trade, making some presents to them.

Of course the *Nashville American* also ran this story, titling it "How the Bluff on Which Nashville Now Stands was First Discovered by White Men—Thrilling Experiences of the French Traders Over a Century Ago!"

And thus was set in motion a series of tales about Timothy that haunt Nashville today. It's a story full of awesome hyperbolic nonsense, rooted in varying levels of truth. Timothy's wife gives birth in a cave! Timothy stops all Indian attacks! Timothy's wife survives by wrapping herself in a bear's skin! Well, that one, maybe . . . and, perhaps, most interestingly, Timothy survives a gunshot wound from the Battle of the Plains of Abraham! Well, he was just twelve then. And would a young, favorite son of high French Canadian nobility really find himself on a battlefield before his teen years? Though

Montcalm filled his ranks with children as young as fourteen out of desperation, it was unlikely an even-younger son of a nobleman would be called to fight.

3

New France

Let's back up a little.

In the midst of the French-English struggle for territory in and around Quebec, in the ice cold of early spring on the plains of New France, Jacques Timothé Boucher Sieur de Montbreun is born to Jean Etienne Boucher Sieur de Montbrun and Delle Marie Racicot. It's March 23, 1747, at least according to the Catholic Church records of the tiny town of Boucherville, a hamlet a few hours' horse ride north of Montreal, diagonally across the St. Lawrence River. He is their second son.

Timothy's great-grandfather, Pierre Boucher, came from France as a teenager to help settle the new land. Pierre lived among the Iroquois and Jesuit priests, and was well-liked by both sides when he became a translator between the natives and the arriving French. He soon became the assistant to the governor of Trois-Rivières. He was great at both math and wilderness survival, setting an early standard for the kind of wilderness man–meets–Harvard PhD that Timothy would become. Pierre's diplomacy didn't go unnoticed, and he was soon the first to be elevated to nobility in New France (you can find a statue of him today outside the Parliament Building in Quebec). The King of France gifted him with the name of the town, and most of Boucherville's residents were related, living in modest homes set on long, narrow plots that extended from the town center down to the river bank. Pierre's now-noble seed soon began to spread far and wide, and the family, taking on high level fleur-de-lis-approved names such as "de Boucherville," "de Grand-Pre" and "de Niverville," went on to be pivotal in the founding of New Orleans, as well as the states of Mississippi and Florida. Pierre's son Jean picked the name "de Montbrun," translated as "of the brown mountain." Jean's story was complicated because he remarried after his first wife died, and that second wife tied up much of the family fortune in court for years, complicating any legacy due to his sons, Etienne and René. It's nice to see a little foreshadowing here with both the women and the courts. Either way, that second wife in no way wanted any of Jean's money to end up in the hands of the de Montbrun sons, even though she had no children of her own.

Etienne begat Timothy. Etienne served in the local militia under the Marquis de Montcalm, and it was he, not Timothy, who fought on the Plains of Abraham against the British. Though Montcalm was famously killed, Etienne was wounded and survived. Timothy was no stranger to violence and death as a youngster: twelve of his fourteen siblings died young, leaving only his two sisters. Those two chose a life even closer to the family's devout Catholicism: both became Grey Nun nurses at a hospital in Montreal.

When Timothy was sixteen, New France was no more. With the Treaty of 1763, England assumed control of the land he called home. Until then, he may have felt a familiar pull toward the militia, but with New France in ruins, he leaned into the perhaps more exciting stories of his uncles and cousins who had explored the areas to the south and west that we now know as the Dakotas, Iowa, Minnesota and even the Rocky Mountains. He listened intently to tales of his uncle Pierre Boucher DeMontbrun de la Soudraye, head of the militia at Kaskaskia in the Illinois Territory. The wild, far reaches of the French frontier were calling.

At age nineteen, he fell in love with Marguerite Thérèse-Archange Gibault, hereafter referred to as Therese, also of nobility. She was the daughter of Etienne Gibault, who died before the marriage, and Marie Catherine Dubois, who had remarried a successful local merchant who knew all the town gossip, including Timothy's talk of leaving Boucherville. Marie did not like Timothy and argued incessantly to call off the nuptials. Marie knew Timothy was restless, and that her daughter, used to the comforts of high society, would not fare well on the rivers and in the forests of the "untamed frontier savages."

Nonetheless, they married on November 26, 1766. Though Timothy was just nineteen, their wedding certificate noted that the two had been in love for a long time—shocking, since Therese, born June 19, 1751, was only fifteen. That wedding certificate indicated it wasn't necessarily a fairytale romance; normally, a direct family member would be present, but in this case, a cousin was needed to condone the proceedings as no more-immediate relative was willing.

> Were present Mr. Thimothe Boucher, Esquire, Lord of Montbrun, son of Mr. Etienne Boucher, Esquire, and of Marie Racicot, his father and mother, living in Boucherville Manor and stipulating for himself and in his name, party of the first part,
>
> And Miss Marguerite Archange Gibault, daughter of Mr. Etienne Gibault and of Mrs. Dubois, actual wife of Mr. Pierre Reaume, business man, living in Boucherville, party of the second part:
>
> Both parties having said that they have been in love for a long time and the beautiful Gibault (girl) finding opposition to her marriage with Mr. Boucher, who, in order to succeed in it, is about to have recourse to the authority of the gentlemen Justices of the Peace of His Majesty in this city, consequently cannot have the consent of said gentlemen—Mrs. Reaume having had stipulated the articles and conventions that they wish to have executed, nevertheless said parties finding that they were sufficiently authorized to contract said marriage, despite the lack of consent of Mr. and Mrs. Reaume . . .

Therese's mother did not like Timothy and is rumored to have begged her to not marry him. The certificate continued that the parties would equally share real estate and other belongings and that if Timothy died first Therese would inherit all of his property and a security income fund. It adds more, as "proof of their love":

> And as the parties wish to give to each other certain proofs of their reciprocal love, they have made and they make each other by this document entire donation, pure and reciprocal, of all of the wealth, buildings and real estate acquired or to be acquired, in such a manner that said wealth be owed to and acquired by the survivor of the two; said survivor is to accept whatever will have belonged to the first deceased, at the day of his death, provided that at said day there are no children or will not be any from said marriage, otherwise the present donation will be nullified, but will again be in force if said children were to die in minority or before being provided by marriage, all in case that said donation take place, to enjoy by said survivor from the benefit of it as his own property and to use as he pleases, as well as [his heir who causes?], for such is the wish of these parties, who, as proof of their own consent to the present agreement despite all opposition and lack of parents of said wife, have signed in Boucherville this twenty-sixth day of November One Thousand Seven Hundred Sixty-Six . . .

Within two years, Therese was pregnant and Timothy was more than ready to leave. Their fervor and faith in a new world was enough to propel them, plus one unborn child, out of the comfort of Boucherville, and down the rivers to a brave new world.

4

A River Runs through It

Between March and October 1768, Timothy and Therese travelled more than 2,200 miles by water from Boucherville to Kaskaskia, the capital of the Illinois Territory. They spent most of their days on a lake or a river, with the company of Therese's cousin, Pierre, (yes, Father Gibault, the one who gave them permission to marry) and his sister and mother. It was a smart time to travel, these warmer months of the year—it was wise that they left Boucherville as soon as the ice on the St. Lawrence began to weaken. Historians somewhat agree on a logical route: the St. Lawrence southwest through many of the Great Lakes, then along the Niagara and Detroit Rivers, where they navigated falls and drops and currents as fast as thirty miles per hour. They enjoyed the scenery from four or five large wooden canoes known as pirogues, designed with flat bottoms so they could be easily dragged instead of carried.

The pirogues were packed with supplies, including animal traps, flints, long bows and arrows, and guns and ammunition. It is believed two oxen rode in one canoe, so they could pull everything across land during portages. The guns required some work; the party had to find saltpeter for ammunition in limestone caves to mix with charcoal and form gunpowder. Guns and water usually meant rust, so great care was taken to keep both guns and gunpowder high and dry. The travelers lived off the land and cooked over a fire, hunting and foraging for food and clothing and using pine pitch to repair boat leaks. There was always a risk of native attack, either on water, where the native birch bark canoes were faster and easier to maneuver; or, on land at night, where letting down one's guard to sleep or bathe could be disastrous. Timothy already spoke several native languages, a skill that likely saved his life many times, beginning on this very first expedition. The group likely stopped at every native trading post along the rivers, checking on Catholic missions, and making sure everyone was working hard at being Catholic.

By August, they reached their first main portage, near what is now Niles, Michigan. There, at a trading post called

Fort St. Joseph, which was a Potawatomi-Miami native village, Therese gave birth to their first child, Agnes. Natives assisted in the birth, and Agnes was immediately baptized. It was August 18, 1768. The travelers decided to rest for a week in the company of the hundreds of trappers, natives, and hunters at the trading post. In the heat of the fading summer, the party of six packed up again. They might have made a few notes on an animal skin: which branch of a river to take, where to overnight, where the natives might be more prone to attack. They floated down the St. Joseph to the Kankakee River before a twenty-five-mile portage over land to the Tippecanoe River, which drains into the Wabash. This marked an especially joyous moment for the group, who for the first time would be travelling in the direction of a river's current. The Wabash led them straight to Vincennes, Indiana for another rest.

Timothy had family in Vincennes, and Pierre had numerous children and adults to baptize, the completion of which led to a huge feast, a rare moment when musical instruments were brought out of hiding and wine was shared. After a few days of rest and civilization, the party was back on the Wabash, paddling toward the Ohio River. Here, their route is debated. Some say they joined the Ohio, turning west to its confluence with the Mississippi River. The last part thus seems almost ridiculous, as they would have turned north at the Mississippi for an arduous seventy-five-mile stretch upriver to Kaskaskia. A Wabash—Little Wabash—Kaskaskia River path may have been the longer but easier route.

In Kaskaskia, Timothy and crew were welcomed with open arms by the three thousand-ish people who called it home. Though now in English hands, the town had remained decidedly French in both appearance and affect since its founding by Jesuit priests some seven decades prior. With nepotism on his side, Timothy asked his Kaskaskian uncle for a home, which he was given—but soon the new residents realized the town was not at all what they expected. Though England was making an attempt to revive the local economy, the people were poor and food was scarce. Timothy soon realized that staying in Kaskaskia would not be the wisest choice for his family or himself. With a new, well-built Philadelphia-financed pirogue, he started to explore farther and farther away from Kaskaskia in search of game, mostly deer, buffalo, and bear. His success as a hunter and trapper made him increasingly popular in Kaskaskia. By 1770, Timothy had been named justice of the peace, and Therese was pregnant again. On February 12, 1770, their second son, Timothe Félix (hereafter referred to as Felix), was born.

Timothy's justice of the peace work strengthened his skills at managing a land in full political chaos. There was constant discord among the English, French, Spanish, and the native tribes. Arguably, Kaskaskia's path toward ignominy was already in place, which provided fuel to the fire of Timothy's desire to explore opportunities farther and farther away. By 1770, his trips were numerous and long.

Strangely, in 1772, Therese dropped out of any known public record, a ghost to history until either 1780 or 1783 (sources disagree). There are theories that she was captured by natives and taken to the Dakotas. Her mysterious disappearance may have affected Timothy's decisions as his reach expanded farther south to New Orleans to trade furs, and deeper to the southeast, as he moved through Kentucky into a fertile hunting ground around the Cumberland River in what is now north central Tennessee.

5

Cave Man

Timothy was a master of the rivers, running the Mississippi, Ohio, and Illinois, eventually heading farther south to the unexplored Cumberland to trap game. Among the looping bends of that river, he found a salt lick frequented by game (this area became known as Sulphur Dell, today it's the site of the Bicentennial Mall) and set up an outpost, taking full advantage of this Shawnee, Chickasaw, and Creek Nation hunting, fishing, and burial crossroads. It's likely he had heard about the game in this region from his family, particularly from his uncles who had spent a great deal of time fur trapping in the region. The geography, especially the central bluff above the river, and the previous trading posts that had been set up by the Shawnee, made it a perfect focal point for trading with the natives. He planned to split his time between this new place and Kaskaskia, and to make the trip several times a year.

According to the William Alexander Provine papers (which seem to be full of half-clues and shadows of everything that was really going on in Timothy's life, thanks to plenty of unclear or half-finished letters and ideas), Timothy began to hunt and explore the area around the Cumberland River in the early 1770s. By 1774, Timothy had eight boats and seventeen men in his employ, and Katherine Demonbreun Whitefort recorded in her history that he built his first cabin for storage of furs and tallow on the banks of the Cumberland River at Nashville that same year.

But it is Josephus Conn Guild's story of the day Timothy's "discovered" what would become Nashville that set the legend in motion. In his 1878 book *Old Times in Tennessee,* Guild gave us a melodramatic retelling of events, setting a narrative that has blurred the lines between fact and fiction ever since.

> They ran up what is now Lick Branch . . . and tied up their boat . . . DeMonbreun wore a blue cotton hunting shirt, leggings of deer-hide, a red waistcoat that had once been in the French army and a fox-skin cap, with the tail hanging down his back. He was a tall, athletic, dark-skinned man, with a large head, broad shoulders and chest, small legs, a high, short foot, an eagle eye, and an expression of daring about his mouth. His followers addressed him as Jacques. They concluded to trace the

FIGURE 5. The river entrance to Demonbreun's cave is still visible across the Cumberland River from Shelby Park in East Nashville. Photo courtesy of William Alexander Provine Papers, 1552–1935, Tennessee Historical Society Collection, Tennessee State Library and Archives, Nashville, Tennessee.

> stream in which their boat was then lying to its source, and as they followed its meanderings, they noticed a movement among the bushes . . . One of the men lowered his gun but DeMonbreun ordered him not to shoot, as their object was to trade and not make war.

One of the most enduring Timothy myths, one touted by generations of historians from Joseph Conn Guild to Harriette Arnow, is that during this time a fox-skin-cap-wearing Timothy lived in a cave above the Cumberland River. It was a secret place safe from native attack and a perfect place for his mistress to have their child.

Arnow believed the cave was somewhere between Mill Creek and Stone's River, placing it on the east side of Nashville. This cave had a long ladder for access, one that Timothy pulled into the cave after he settled in for the evening. Today, there is a cave in this location, now on private property, that has been so often thought of as "Demonbreun's Cave" that it even received an official historic marker from the state of Tennessee. This cave has one entrance above the river, and another land entrance a few thousand feet inland. Not many Nashvillians today have seen the cave, but if you stand in the right spot at Shelby Bottoms Park you can see the entrance above the swirling currents. (You can also sneak around Cave Road and Omohundro Road on the south bank, climb down a rotting set of stairs, hang over the side of the rocky bank, and shimmy over, dodging bats leaving at dusk, to peer into Timothy's supposed quarters.) It's the only property in the city listed on the National Register of Historic Places that requires a boat trip to access legally.

We know a few things for sure about Nashville's history at the time. French game trappers were coming in and out of the area, alongside a few long hunters from Virginia. The long hunters were men from the New and Holston Rivers region of Virginia who made expeditions into the British colonial frontier wilderness of present-day Kentucky and Tennessee for as much as six months at a time. Much like Timothy's winter hunting schedule, this was an October to April affair. These men were Scots-Irish, mostly Protestant, a stark contrast to the French-speaking Catholic who also hunted around the salt lick.

One thing these men had in common, however, was a tendency to want a woman in both locations: one at home, and another at the hunting grounds. For French fur traders like Timothy, that woman was often a native, someone who could speak the language and generally ease arguments and handle discussions with native tribes much more easily than a lone Frenchmen with a gun and a desire to share the meat and hides. A partner who had safe passage through the native lands meant less-risky travel.

Timothy's time in the cave was not likely spent alone. He had a woman in the cave with him and they had a baby with blue-gray eyes, named William. The year of William's birth is difficult to confirm with any accuracy, with a wild swing of 1784 to 1794 depending on the source. But wife Therese was back home in Kaskaskia, or a captive off in the Dakotas, either way now likely battle-scarred after numerous incidents with various natives and/or raising at least three of Demonbreun's other children. The cave was simply his Nashville home, and the woman, Elizabeth Bennett (likely born Elizabeth Himslar,

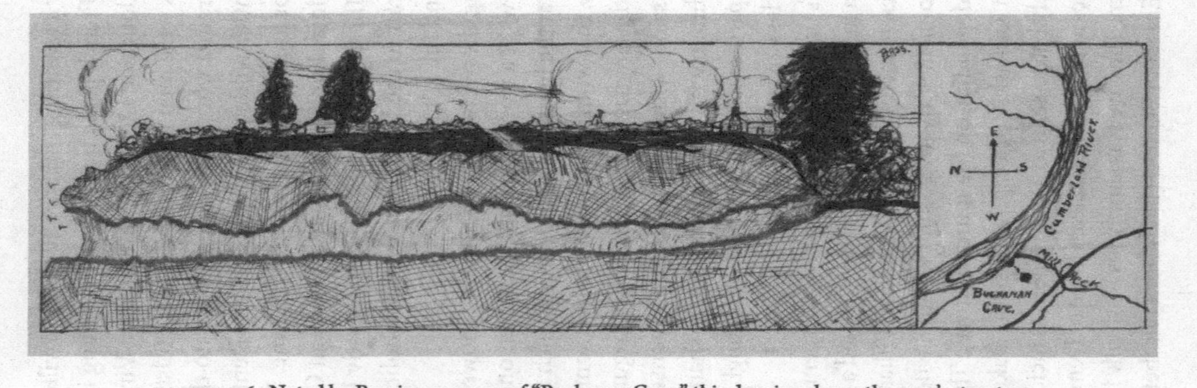

FIGURE 6. Noted by Provine as a map of "Buchanan Cave," this drawing shows the cave's structure. Image courtesy of William Alexander Provine Papers, 1552–1935, Tennessee Historical Society Collection, Tennessee State Library and Archives, Nashville, Tennessee.

but who might have married someone named Bennett prior to meeting Timothy), was either a mistress or a second wife.

Nobody truly knows Elizabeth's story before she met Demonbreun. Who she is, how she got there, how they met, and what those two were really doing in a damp, musty stone room fifteen feet above the racing Cumberland remains unclear. It is unlikely she could read or write, and she left no written trace of her thoughts or motivation. She may have come to the area with an English exploratory party from, one, her birthplace in Virginia (corroborated with a later census as her home state) and she may have been half Choctaw; or, two, from her birthplace in North Carolina, making it more likely she was half Cherokee. Her gravestone gives her a birthdate of July 24, 1740. It also lists her death as 1856, making her 116 years old, but we'll get into that later.

We may never know if, or for how long, the pair lived in the cave. When a flotilla of English settlers led by James Robertson arrived in 1779 and built what came to be known as Fort Nashborough, Timothy already had an adjacent trading post, and soon set up more traditional housing "in town." Family rumors today indicate he may have kept Elizabeth in the cave since the English did not approve of the affair.

Not everybody, however, buys the cave story. Davidson County historian Carole Bucy can't make the pieces fit.

"I haven't heard that much that is flatly wrong about Timothy," she said. "These are stories that have been handed down so they are rooted in the truth. Except the cave. I simply don't think a woman could have lived there and given birth in it. Even the river was lower then, making it even more preposterous. Instead, I think he camped there."

FIGURE 7. Above ground at the McNairy Vault in the City Cemetery on Fourth Avenue, south of downtown Nashville. Some say it covers the entrance to a once-important cave. Photo by author.

Bucy pointed out that part of the myth is bolstered by the fact that this cave is the only cave still visible in Nashville today. In Timothy's time, there were caves all over the city. In fact, there is a cave rumored to be accessible through what is now the McNairy family vault at the City Cemetery, a cave that once was easily visible from Second Avenue South.

"Nashville is on a bed of limestone, full of caves, and there are pockets on it," she continued. "I think he could have lived in a cave, but because the one we see today has remained so visible it became his cave. He came in by following the river, so it's highly likely he camped along the cave, as shelter, but even that could have been the cave near Second Avenue. So much has changed now, of course."

Provine's papers line up with Bucy's theory: Provine claimed it was Guild who bolstered the story, and the only mention of a cave prior to that is in a brief account Timothy's son wrote for a friend, where he indicated his father took refuge in a cave for a week after being "chased by Indians." In 1957, Wirt agreed cave life was impossible:

> This William, the youngest of all Demonbreun's children, is one who is invariably named . . . as the "cave baby." One has only to consider situation in Nashville in 1794 [debatable as others place William's birth a decade earlier], when the town was a decade from its more primitive character, and the fact that at this Timothy Demonbreun is known to have been living on lower College Street to realize the impossibility of the story. As a matter of fact, there has probably never been a year that the cave was not submerged one or more times by the river, and one is forced to the conclusion that Timothy's connection with the cave goes no further than his son's statement that once he took temporary refuge in it when pursued by Indians.

The official family history, *The Forgotten Frenchman* by Truman Weldon De Munbrun, romanticized that a pregnant-with-their-third-child Therese joined Timothy on his second trip to the Cumberland. He wanted a safe place for her to stay while he was out trapping and trading, so he found the cave for Therese and the two were simply delighted when they discovered that the smoke from a fire would exit the cave in a way that nobody could see, making it even safer from attack. Within days, a baby named William was born and he was thus the first white child born in what is now Middle Tennessee. The pair plus infant then quickly returned to Kaskaskia. De Munbrun puts an asterisk at the end of this paragraph, which leads to a one-word note at the bottom of the page: "*Supposition." And he was wrong. William was not Therese's child.

But Timothy as cave man is still the legend that persists most. It's a big, brave tale that matches the à la mode Davy Crockett persona the family prefers. In fact, though he declined to be interviewed for this book, one young male descendent of the Demonbreun line (currently in his thirties) is known to take girlfriends to visit a string of caves up and down the Cumberland near Nashville, to "connect to his past and who he is" because, he explained, it's in his blood.

For the original Demonbreun, both on the Cumberland and in Kaskaskia, things were getting complicated fast—not only in his love life, but between the nations who wanted to control the frontier lands, and with a new country who wanted its independence.

6

A Tale of Two Cities

For nearly two decades, from the early 1770s to 1790, Timothy essentially lived in two places. He spoke English and French and numerous native dialects. The rivers were his highways. The balance of his wild freedom on the waterways changed significantly, however, with the Revolutionary War. It took almost three years for the shots fired at Lexington to echo across the Mississippi, when, on the ironic date of July 4, 1778, revolutionary Colonel George Rogers Clark marched into and occupied Kaskaskia without a fight.

Sixteen days later, Timothy, perhaps sensing the Americans had a brighter future than the Spanish or French, swore allegiance to the United States at nearby Fort Vincennes. Also on the list of the 128 Frenchman who pledged themselves to the American cause was a man named Joseph Derrat, a friend of Timothy's who would later play an intriguing role in his Nashville life, both civic and romantic. Joseph Derrat: remember that name.

Then things got sideways in the war. By December, British general Henry Hamilton seized Fort Vincennes. Timothy was interesting enough for Hamilton to mention in his journal; in fact, he claimed Timothy said the Americans misled him into taking an oath. Hamilton called his bluff when he asked him to force his French friends to build blockhouses, which Timothy did. It's likely Timothy was simply spying for the Americans, as word of Hamilton's troops and plans quickly made it back to Clark in Kaskaskia through a friend of Timothy's. It's a worthy example of Timothy's skilled political maneuvering.

In a predictable exchange for his loyalty, Timothy was quickly named lieutenant governor of the Illinois territory. The record indicates he was a reliable, fearless leader, trusted by many. "He behaved himself as a friend to the cause of America in every respect," the American army noted. He even was one of only twelve volunteers to defend Fort Jefferson, and was briefly held captive by the British.

Around this time, Therese showed back up in the Kaskaskia records. In fact, the Draper papers indicate he and Therese may have travelled back to Canada, and on the return trip they were attacked by natives, who killed everyone else in the party, leaving only Timothy and his wife out of respect for his legend. However, Draper concluded, the natives took everything they had except the clothes on their back. The pair made a raft out of logs and grapevines and floated down the river to safety. This Canada trip is not mentioned elsewhere.

These other trips, and his work as lieutenant governor, meant his trips to the Cumberland were few and far between. It's of note that things get chronologically very challenging around this time. In 1782, he ran for office in Kaskaskia, but only got one vote. He was on a (likely trading) trip to New Orleans in 1776. In 1777, he's in Vincennes. In 1778, Kaskaskia and Vincennes. But things get dicey with documentation, often indicating he's in Nashville and Kaskaskia at almost the same time. This travel would all be by river or horseback, meaning these trips were epic and slow, requiring weeks or months at times between locations. In a nascent Nashville, Timothy is in court records "retailing liquor without a license," while around the same time he requested reimbursement from the Virginia government for travel from Kaskaskia to Cahokia. Also in this same time period, he handled trouble with the Spanish governor, Francisco Cruzat, who illegally seized two Spanish refugees from American asylum in Kaskaskia. The deftness of Timothy's letter to Cruzat arguably prevented a larger-scale conflict between Spain and the fledgling United States. Cruzat really liked the guy—he later offered Timothy a home in St. Louis and an officer position in the Spanish army. The Spanish empire had designs on the trans-Appalachia settlements, and recognized Timothy's influence in the area. This offer was likely a courting of sorts for him to be a part of their attempt to secure lands east of the Mississippi for King Charles III. This was not the end of their attempts to work with Timothy. But at this point in his life, he had enough going on and declined.

He was ready to decline a lot. On August 14, 1786, at Kaskaskia, he resigned as lieutenant governor. His resignation offered simply "best wishes for his successor." Perhaps there was too much conflict between American Kaskaskia and the French who still lived there. Kaskaskia, incidentally, was also beginning its century-long, flood-driven disappear-under-the-Mississippi-River act. There's an 1848 newspaper article that hinted Timothy killed a man in a duel and had to leave Kaskaskia. Of course, duel killings were pretty amped up in the mid-nineteenth century, so that incident remains hearsay. But, regardless of the cause, in that moment, Timothy chose Nashville.

Carole Bucy called this an interesting choice.

"There's no Catholic Church in Nashville," she explained. "A priest had to come down from Bardstown, Kentucky, to take confession, which is odd because you don't really think of Catholic priests as circuit riders like the Methodists. Because religion was so important to Timothy the simple fact that he comes back to Nashville to live is pretty interesting. When the English took the French territory, many Frenchman crossed the Mississippi and built Genevieve, taking their chances with the Spanish Empire, not the English. But Timothy doesn't. Maybe he felt he had a great deal in common with the Scots-Irish who were coming to middle Tennessee.

"They all came for opportunity. Once the town was settled this was about as good a place to be a land speculator as any. Maybe Timothy wouldn't have considered himself a land speculator, but he did want to buy for a low price, sell, and move on. But he must have liked it as well, and the fact that his descendants stuck around is further testament to that."

Land was quickly becoming the name of the game. In 1787, Timothy received his first land grant, more than one thousand acres in Montgomery County, Tennessee (near the Cheatham County line) as payment for his Revolutionary War services. In April 1788, about seven months later, Timothy sold the land to his son-in-law, Jacques Chenier, still in Kaskaskia—who had married his now twenty-year-old first daughter, Agnes. A year later, Timothy and Therese had their last child, Marie-Louise.

By 1790, he had opened a tavern in a stone building near Nashville's Public Square. His two families, including now five children with Therese and potentially at least two with Elizabeth, were about to occupy the same geography permanently.

7

Your Cheatin' Heart; or, "It's Complicated" at Lot 45

One of the most enduring myths about Timothy is that he was a bigamist. That he had, at least, one long-term affair with a woman named Elizabeth. He doesn't hide this: their children are openly listed in his will. But the timing of his relationship with Elizabeth and whether or not Therese disappeared are key factors that remain shrouded in a dubious timeline and gossipy half-truths. There's no doubt Therese disappeared, but the how, when, and why of that disappearance remain a mystery. Wirt summarized what happened almost too succinctly:

> Beginning with the baptism of her son, [Therese] appears frequently in the records at Kaskaskia, either bearing or presenting for baptism children of her own, or acting as godmother for other's children. Then, after her appearance at the baptism of her youngest child on May 22, 1790, she drops abruptly from sight.
>
> Considering the fact that the family was Catholic, and the civil and ecclesiastical records of Kaskaskia are virtually complete, it seems unlikely that there could have been a divorce. Perhaps she had died, and it is even possible that she came with him from Nashville.

But he has that wrong. Therese disappeared much earlier, around 1772—and is gone from the record until around 1783, as discussed earlier. She and Timothy had five children, two before 1772 and then three starting fifteen years later (Julienne, Timothy Jr., and Marie-Louise). In the meantime, and perhaps before, Elizabeth and Timothy were romantically involved. And that's the heart of one of the biggest Timothy legends—his affair with Elizabeth: when did it start, why did it happen, and what the hell was really going on? There were plenty of children from both. To further add to the mystery is Lot 45, a one-acre square of land "with all the buildings and improvements" on lower College Street (now Third Ave-

FIGURE 8. A plaque at the corner of today's Broadway and Third Avenue in downtown Nashville commemorates the original Lot 45. Photo by author.

nue) in the new town of Nashville, that changed hands several times between Timothy and Elizabeth, setting a strange example of land wheeling and dealing that may at its heart have more to do with his romantic affairs than love ever did.

So who was he having children with and when? Table 1 gives us a clear understanding of the overlap of the two relationships. Demonbreun family historians often erroneously list William's birth as 1794, likely based on the incorrect date on William's gravestone. The date discrepancy may also be an easy attempt to defend Elizabeth's presence, remarking that Timothy surely thought his wife had died at the hands of natives, and he remarried accordingly. However, an examination of his will (which stated William is an illegitimate child) and an objective view of the children's birthdates leaves

Table 1. Demonbreun's children and their mothers

Birth Year	*with Therese*	*with Elizabeth*	*with Martha Gray*
1768	Therese Agnes	—	—
1770	Felix	—	—
1785	Julienne	—	—
1784–86	—	William	—
1788	Timothy Jr.	John Baptiste	—
1789	Marie-Louise	—	Unknown boy
1792	—	Polly	Unknown girl

no room for defense. In fact, it makes more sense for Timothy to have had a child with Elizabeth in Nashville in 1784 if you want to stick to that "he-thought-Therese-was-dead" alibi, as he technically could have gotten Elizabeth pregnant before Therese showed back up in 1783. Nonetheless, based on census records, Williams was likely born between 1784 and 1786. Elizabeth and Timothy were brought to court for "having a bastard child" in January 1787. Later court records indicate William did not know his true birth date.

But Therese was soon back, and joined Timothy and co. in Nashville. That didn't seem to trouble his libido. In 1788, in fact, he fathered children with both women. Sometime before, he and Elizabeth had left the alleged cave behind for a house in the new town, which developed on a ridge north and west of the cave. He acquired several lots, including Lot 45. There are rumors he tried to marry Elizabeth around this time but that the marriage was denied by the court.

Timothy and Therese, as you recall, moved to Nashville full-time in 1786. So, for at least six years, Elizabeth and Therese were both in Nashville, and both having Timothy's children. Elizabeth takes the fall for their actions at least once, in 1787 as the aforementioned city court records showed, when she was tried for having a bastard.

The Provine papers got really exciting here:

> Timothy Demonbreun lived also with a woman by the name of Crutcher, by whom he had no children. [He] also lived with Martha [Patsy] Gray, [who was an aunt of Wm Bennett], by whom he had two children—a boy and a girl. They were quite small when Bennett visited them & does not know what became of them, he thinks this woman was from Georgia. (brackets in original)

Provine concluded by stating that Timothy lived with three women as "common-law wives" in addition to Therese.

According to many accounts, in 1791, Timothy's two-year-old daughter by Therese, Mary-Louise, was killed in a raid, stolen from Therese's arms and scalped in front of her as the two tried to escape via horseback. After this, Therese disappeared from city records, dying either from heartbreak, illness, or utter exhaustion. There is no official record of when or where she died; some say that Timothy took her all the way back to her family in Boucherville. Her mother, if still alive, might have reminded her how much she disliked Timothy, and how hard she fought to prevent the wedding.

Elizabeth, however, had a different destiny. She also had money. In February that same year, she bought property

FIGURE 9. Buchanan's Station circa 1936. The log building in the foreground is a remnant of the original fort, while the house to the left dates from the early nineteenth century. Photo courtesy of Garden Study Club of Nashville Collection, Tennessee State Library and Archives, Nashville, Tennessee.

FIGURE 10. The site of Buchanan's Station, at the intersection of Elm Hill Pike and Massman Drive, is now an office park. As of 2021, only the cemetery remains high along the banks of Mill Creek. Photo by author.

from Timothy—Lot 164. A few months later, on July 7, 1791, he sold her Lot 45.

The next year, according to historians Doug Drake, Jack Masters, and Bill Puryear, she made bullets during the raid at Buchanan's Station, fighting alongside Timothy and the other white men. Remember Joseph Derrat from the make-your-oath-to-the-new-America days back in Vincennes? He was also trapped in the raid.

Something must have changed there, or soon thereafter, as Elizabeth married Joseph in March 1793 (that date dispels the rumors that Timothy married Elizabeth off to his friend Joseph because Therese was coming to town). These two had children in 1793, 1794, and 1795. There are rumors some of these offspring were fathered by Timothy—and there are local stories that say Timothy was asked by city leaders to end his polygamist ways if he wanted to be part of the town, so he married one wife off to his best friend in an attempt to gain more political and social power. It's also possible they had an "it's complicated"-style relationship, where Timothy continued to be involved with Elizabeth, and her marriage to Joseph simply made sense for everybody involved—in particular socially and politically.

But things get even stranger. Timothy bought Lot 45 back from Elizabeth and Joseph on June 1, 1793. Things get wilder as Elizabeth owned Timothy's tavern for two years and Joseph spread rumors that the Spanish were preparing to attack the city, which proved false. Elizabeth, Joseph, and Timothy passed land back and forth, back and forth. In 1797, Timothy sold Elizabeth ninety-two acres listed only as "north of the Cumberland River" with an important provision that "her husband could not dispose of it."

Elizabeth was clearly something out of the ordinary, especially for her time.

8

The Other Woman

So who is this Elizabeth Bennett, Himslar—eventually Derrat? The historic record is regrettably lean, and rife with rumors from her beginnings (Cherokee?!) to her longevity (116 years old?!). But one thing stands above all else. It's clear Timothy needed her. Whether she was a knowledge-able, skilled woman who made perfect sense as a partner on the frontier or a star-crossed true love is guesswork. But we have a few clues to who she was. She is often referred to as his "common law" wife.

She likely came from Virginia or North Carolina, perhaps with an early English settler, or the long hunters. She may have been part native, perhaps Cherokee or Creek—but it is of note that, at the time, women on the frontier who lived like natives were treated as and called native. It was also somewhat customary for French fur traders and the long hunters to take a "second woman" along the frontier.

Provine indicated Elizabeth first had children with a man with the last name Bennett, then another man named Himslar or Hensley, and of course, Timothy and then Joseph. She may have also had children with another man named Cagle after that (this seems incorrect as Timothy and Elizabeth's child Polly married a Cagle, and Timothy and Therese's child Felix also married a Cagle, but you never know). This string of men and children seems improbable considering the social norms of the day, leaving another question mark about her character. Historian Betsy Phillips wondered if "she already had a social status that gave her access to a lot of men but left them unsurprised when she got pregnant with someone else's child." Could Elizabeth have been a professional "other woman"? Some sources theorize that she was having Timothy's and Joseph's children in alternating years.

Timothy didn't seem to have a problem with the various fathers, though. In fact, he sold land to one of her children by another man. In 1793, Philis (also referred to as Philix) Theodore Bennett purchased Lot 164 from Timothy:

> Between Timothy Demunbre of Davidson County and Territory of the United States south of the river Ohio of

> the one part and Philis Theodore Bennett son of Elizabeth Bennett, commonly called Hinslar of the said County and territory of the other Part. Witnesseth that the said Timothy Demombre for and in consideration of the sum of one-hundred dollars to him in hand paid the receipt whereof he doth by these presents acknowledge.

Imagine the relationship between Therese and Elizabeth. They were both in Nashville for three to four years, perhaps many more, but there is no clear record of who lived with whom and where, and whether the two were amicable or arch enemies. Timothy often did things for Elizabeth and her offspring (his or otherwise), whether in land trades or in court. She stepped up in return, including running his downtown tavern. His relationship with her was never secret. One could suppose Therese left town because of Elizabeth, but that's simple soap-opera style speculation. Was there a moment where Timothy said to Elizabeth, "baby, my wife is still alive and she's coming to town"? At the same time, did he sheepishly (or proudly) confess to Therese, "mon petit chou, there's this woman in Nashville who has a bunch of my children, and we're moving there, so can we all just get along"?

There is no doubt Elizabeth was a necessity for Timothy early on. It's possible she spoke native languages, perhaps some local to the Cumberland area that Timothy was unfamiliar with. All of their children received Timothy's family names (William, Batteaste/Baptiste, and Polly). It is likely, and we will explore this further on, that she returned to Timothy when Joseph died—indicating perhaps more than just a need, but a strong love between the two. It is quite unlikely, however, that she was Catholic, which must have been problematic.

Elizabeth signed bills of sales with illegible scrawl or an X, indicating she likely did not know how to read or write. That did not stop her from buying and selling property alone in the eighteenth century, not a common feat for a woman. One could argue Timothy was sending her money from Kaskaskia, but no record of that has been found (yet). She was perhaps, as Phillips also speculated, "a bawdy woman from the get-go," which means she may have owned a tavern or dealt in drink from the beginning, given her own spending money. She did well, and long after Timothy's star faded, she had her own place, known as Granny Rat's Tavern. Likely the "Rat" came from a shortened version of the last name Durrat.

When the tavern building sold in the 1830s, it was described as a huge stone building and a horse barn. It had fourteen fireplaces and sat six hundred feet south of the split of Clarksville Pike and the road to Springfield (now White's Creek Pike). Based on its construction, it must have been expensive to build. Some called it an inn or a tavern, others referred to it as a "bawdy house." A little detective work on the map today places this near the location of the Anderson-Garrett Funeral Home in Joelton, in the rolling hills northwest of Nashville. Though that building has been modified many times, the center portion still retains a ghost of a building, both in foyer and window placement, that indicates it could certainly be from that time period. There are also curious indentations, stones and depressions in the field out front that could, if viewed at just the right angle, be described as the footprint of an older building.

Even with limited information, it's not a stretch to say Elizabeth was a badass. A rarity in her day and age: a property owner, tavern proprietor, bullet maker / Indian fighter and frontier wild card. She was a perfect foil for Timothy, a match to his charm and wit, a challenge to his intellect and business acumen—and most likely a perfect partner in a land abruptly changed from remote river wilderness to a busy new American town. She was likely wise beyond her centuries, a willing part of Timothy's adventure as well as his duplicitous affairs.

9

The Spy Who Shagged Me

Timothy knew his way around diplomacy, duplicitous or benign. He corresponded with the literal bigwigs: Alexander Hamilton, then secretary of treasury, and Thomas Jefferson, then governor of Virginia, and he traveled to both Williamsburg and Philadelphia on government business. He is often remembered, though, through the lens of the victors of the new world. An example, from our grand myth-making biography *The Forgotten Frenchman*:

> Timothy was well aware that some tribes were not to be trusted and were a real and constant threat to the more civilized and peace loving tribes. It was this basic characteristic that proved in future years to be the key to his success in business and arbitration with the Indians so often required for the protection of the early settlers.

It is likely that Timothy knew how to negotiate wisely with the native tribes, though they may have many darker stories that will never be told. The fact that Timothy was nearly killed by natives on the Arkansas River in 1776 indicated his skills were not always effective.

Timothy exhibited deft skill (political, legal, and personal) when dealing with the complexity of dueling nations, European and native. This skill is interestingly demonstrated in an example that lends credence to his work as a spy. In 1777, British governor Edward Abbott employed Timothy as his "confidential messenger" from Vincennes. At the time, the British were instigating native attacks on white settlements in Kentucky. Abbott sent Timothy to Middle Tennessee to contact Tory families living on the Cumberland. Timothy told the Tories they were not safe, and suggested relocation to the British-held Illinois territory. Of course, General Clark stepped in at this time to take Vincennes, and Timothy immediately pledged allegiance to the United States, then double-crossed the British when he shared British plans with Clark. Where did his heart lie? One cannot imagine he felt much loyalty to the British, who had ravaged his family and homeland back in

Canada. Perhaps he wanted the Tories out of Nashville regardless. But his next move, to double-cross the British for the sake of brand new America, and to execute that double-cross with dexterity and grace, indicated he was intellectually skilled enough to be an effective spy. Today, we might say he had great emotional intelligence as well. The British were done with Timothy. The Americans, however, were sold. Exhibit A, a letter to General Clark extolling Timothy's dedication:

> To all Home It May Consarn,
>
> This May Certefy that Lt Mumbron haith Beheaved him Self as a Frend to the Cause of America in Evey Respect and that he haith Been Readey at all Times on Eaney immergencey to do Evey thing in his Power for the defence of his Cuntrey & at all times When Ever Called on By his Superior or Commanding officer turned out. When the Savages Came in order to Destroy the Cuntrey Last Spring he turned out With the formost to Repulce them. When I was ordered to Go on the Expodition up the Wabash he allso Went with the Greatest Chearfullness and when The Savages attacted Fort Gefferson when I Could Git But twelve Men to Go with Me he a Gain Ventered his life to the Releefe of that post. I Think When all These proofes are Considered that he oute to be aplaused by Evey Good Man and Rewarded Acording to his Merrite.
>
> Geven under My hand
> Jno Montgomery,
> Lt Col Commandant Doc #19

On the bluffs of the Cumberland, politics continued to be complicated. Until 1790, the area was still a part of North Carolina, with the Cumberland plateau separating the settlement from Watauga in East Tennessee, creating a natural barrier that often made the two places feel like separate countries. North Carolina ceded its lands to the federal government in 1790, which created a new no-state's-land called the Southwest Territory until Tennessee statehood six years later. Native attacks remained a constant threat.

"Some people think [James] Robertson was courting the Spanish," explained Bucy. "Timothy could have been a go-between had that happened. There's a chance people in the Cumberland settlement were courting the Spanish before 1790. There were fierce Indian attacks and people living here felt they needed somebody to do something about the Indians. If anything, Timothy could have been an intermediary, but I have not seen that documented."

The Spanish may have been a better option for that protection than the Americans, and safety and security were paramount for the burgeoning city. Since Timothy had already diffused Spanish aggression via an elegant letter from Kaskaskia to Governor Cruzat ("The good understanding and harmony that prevailed 'til now betwixt both Sides of the River of Illinois," he began), his negotiation skills were often sought out in Nashville. The *Territorial Papers of the United States* took note:

> 1792, Sept 15, "Jos. Durat" sees "Old Man Demonbreun" and makes affidavit. The five lower Cherokee towns had declared war against the United States that they

> would be joined by a large number of Creeks and that with their united force they would immediately attack the frontiers of this territory and they were supported by the Spaniards.

On September 30, the tribes attacked Buchanan's Station east of Nashville. Joseph, Timothy's best friend and Elizabeth's husband, warned the city of the attack. Timothy and Joseph knew what was coming—did they know this from the Spanish, or from the tribes themselves? Who trusted them and was betrayed when warning about the attack was given? *Tennessean* reporter Louise Davis confirmed that Timothy later travelled to Williamsburg, Virginia, via horseback, and described the attack to the American Congress.

Records show Timothy is often called on to solve problems, both in and outside of court, in both Kaskaskia and Nashville. His appearances in court are as legendary. He would sue for whatever he felt was correct. In 1787, he was in court more than a dozen times. He was also no stranger to a fight, a reputation that began with stories of conflict in his store. One popular legend is that one fight in the store ended with Timothy tarred and feathered when he took on a much larger man.

In 1789, the "Indian Fighter" John Rains was found guilty of assault and battery against Timothy; it is noted he did Timothy "much harm." The attorney on this case is said to have been Andrew Jackson. It's likely Jackson was Rains' attorney, as Timothy later signed a letter of support in the *Impartial Review and Cumberland Repository* asking the early Nashville newspaper to publish the paper "in mourning" for

Charles Dickinson, whom Jackson killed in a duel. Jackson countered by stating that those who signed the request must have motives based on "something else that at first sight does not appear."

Timothy's wavering allegiances and constant challenges, whether honest or affected, paid off. He received thousands of acres of land grants across Tennessee and Kentucky, all rewards for his loyalty. In a time when land was the name of the game, Timothy won.

10

Granny Rat and Jacques Derrat

He's like the most supporting of all supporting actors, but they constantly mess his name up in the credits so you're left wondering how important this guy was at all—or did the whole storyline actually hinge on his actions and his desires after all?

He's Jacques Derrat/Darrett/Duroque/DuRat/Duratt/Gerrad, et al., depending on the source. Even in brand-new

America, he is soon and often called Joseph. He was one of Timothy's best friends, the man who could marry Elizabeth when Timothy could or would not, and a skilled diplomat / underhanded spy who moved among the French, English, Spanish, American, and native communities with an ease comparable perhaps only to Timothy. On record, Joseph stated that Timothy was, like him, a spy for the Spanish. At a time when the frontier was eyeing either being a part of English-led America, or bleeding into the western boundary of New Spain, it's not illogical that both Timothy and Joseph would err on the Iberian side of things, despite their professed allegiance to the American General Clark.

Eventual Tennessee governor, Andrew Jackson enemy, and all-around Tennessee state "founder" John Sevier wrote:

> Many years past I happened in company with a Frenchman, who lived with the Cherokee and had been a great explorer of the country west of the Mississippi, he informed me that he had been high on the Missouri and traded several months with the Welsh tribe; that they spoke much of the Welsh dialect and although their customs were savage and wild, yet many of them—particularly the females—were very fair and white. [Hold on—what in the world are you talking about, John?] The Frenchman's name has escaped my memory but I believe it was something like Duroque.

Derrat was a mystery man, either from Canada or "half French, half Indian," who appeared occasionally in the frontier record. First, when he joined Timothy to pledge allegiance to the

Americans under Clark at Vincennes, again in the recollection from Sevier, then occasionally in land transactions in Nashville, and most intriguingly, for his role in the natives' raid on Buchanan's Station. Additional letters record that Derrat was a "French militia soldier who became an Indian spy" who reported to Tennessee governor Blount as well as James Robertson.

> Sometime in August preceding the date of the attack... Findleston, a half-breed Cherokee, and one Joseph Durat, a Frenchman, brought information to Nashville—being, as they stated, direct from the Indian Nation—that the Indians were preparing an expedition against Nashville... and intended to make their attack at the next full moon. [Findleston] left the Indian Nation... in company with Durat, under pretense of acting as a spy, in finding out the situation and strength of the defenses about Nashville, and of returning and giving information.

One can assume Joseph and this Findleston spent a lot of time at the "Indian Nation," which was somewhere south of town near the Duck River. They both saw "a large body of Indians" advancing toward Nashville and warned the white settlers of imminent attack—with the additional serious caveat that the natives planned on fully annihilating the white settlement. The Nashvillians heeded their warning and appropriately fortified Buchanan's Station with men and guns. But months passed, and rumors began. People started to believe Joseph made the whole thing up. On September 30, 1792, Buchanan's Station was indeed attacked by the natives, and Timothy, Elizabeth, and Joseph were there to defend it. Elizabeth, alongside other women, helped make bullets. That same year, she gave birth to Polly, her last child with Timothy. But just a few months later, on March 12, 1793, she would forever be known as Elizabeth Hensley Bennett "Gerard" (a.k.a. Durrat) when she married Joseph. The reason for the marriage is a topic of great speculation: was it at Timothy's request? Was it love? Was it convenience? Did Joseph simply get Elizabeth pregnant—hey, what a way to celebrate a win over the natives with the woman who made sure your gun was full of bullets!

Quickly, Joseph and Elizabeth sold Lot 45 back to Timothy. Five years later, Timothy sold the couple ninety-two acres north of town. In that five-year period, Timothy travelled a great deal. He went to Virginia to tell the new American government about the raid, becoming more diplomat than frontiersman. Provine suggested that Elizabeth ran his tavern while he was gone, perhaps explaining why there is overlap of the threesome living at Lot 45. Many of the details of their relationships, romantic and friendship, can only be left to the imagination, though it is clear they trusted each other in business and politics above all else. Sometime during all the Elizabeth-Joseph love, Timothy placed an ad to "buy or rent" a black woman to run his kitchen.

But around the turn of the century, Elizabeth and Joseph left town for the country, where they both ran the infamous Granny Rat's tavern (it's not clear when people started calling her "Granny Rat" rather than Elizabeth, but certainly it's a result of her final last name). The couple had three children and lived in a part of the county now known as Durard

FIGURE 11. Old cabins in Durard Hollow. Photo by author.

Hollow. As of 2020, an old cabin and a small group of tilted gravestones are still visible behind the mid-twentieth-century ranch homes on Ingram Road.

Joseph died around 1808. Elizabeth quickly sold Granny Rat's. Across town, a letter between friends indicated Therese died that same year—coincidence? Elizabeth is soon seen back in town, at Lot 45. Not much is known about her relationship with Timothy from here forward though it is easy to suppose they returned to their romantic ways. In 1812, a Cheatham County boy with the last name Bennett claimed he went to "visit his aunt 'Mrs. Demunbrun' then living at the old fort in Nashville." When Timothy died in 1826, Elizabeth headed northwest once again, to her extended family around Little Marrowbone.

FIGURE 12. The Anderson & Garrett Funeral Home in Joelton may hold clues to the original site of Granny Rat's Tavern. Photo by author.

According to the 1850 census, Elizabeth lived with her grandsons Spencer and Gabriel Demonbrun, sons of John Baptiste. The same census indicates Elizabeth was "born in Virginia," the only honest clue to her origin. Her grandsons and John Baptiste took care of her until she died on February 7, 1856, at the ripe old age of possibly 116 years old (depending on whether you trust the birth year John Baptiste included on her gravestone). That's thirty years of living after Timothy died, during which she was kicked out of Mill Creek Baptist Church for immoral behavior, told wild stories of the days before Nashville, and solidified her status as a Cheatham County legend.

11

Whiskey and Lafayette

We may never know who Timothy lived with and when, and whether Elizabeth was his true love, but we know things changed after the events at Buchanan's Station. Timothy, like Nashville, was settling in—getting older. Though the city had been betrayed by the Spanish during the raid, French relations were good, and in 1797, Timothy was called upon to entertain the three sons of the Duke of Orleans, the oldest of whom would soon be king. There was, according to an early historian, some worry that Timothy was not up to the task of entertaining royalty.

> It appears that DeMonbreun somewhat surprised his fellow townsmen by the common social contract he was able to establish with these higher bred visitors. He was their host during their stay and he gave them the best our metropolis of 300 souls then afforded . . . he asked with starved eagerness about his France and personages and friends he had left there nearly forty years before. He exhibited a treasure of the remote life of his youth: the gold watch and other small articles that he had been able to preserve.

Notably, many of the first historians to write about Timothy assumed he was from France, rather than Canada, and often also assumed the etiquette of his first two decades of near-royal living were completely lost on the frontier.

In 1799, despite his previous charges for retailing liquor without a license, Timothy petitioned the city to pass a law for the building of a market house on the public square, a rapidly growing commercial space where both frame and stone businesses served the sixty to eighty families then living in Nashville. By the next year, Timothy had developed a brisk business there, selling such items as window glass, paper, buffalo tongues, deer hides, and bear grease. He advertised frequently in the newspaper. As that business grew, he asked for a license to keep an ordinary. An ordinary, a colonial forerunner to taverns and inns, was a safe place for travelers to stay.

Timothy's was known for serving good whiskey, and often referred to as the Stone Tavern. An 1811 rental listing in the *Nashville Democrat and Clarion* described it as "a commodious dwelling house in the back yard with three fireplaces; a brick kitchen; a stone meat-house and an elegant two-story stable with a good floor and twenty four good stalls."

Timothy's business expanded beyond the city. He owned a number of carriages, and kept them at Gordon's Ferry, fifty miles south along the Natchez Trace, where John Gordon hosted "twenty or more fancy carriages." He also took great care to keep Nashville clean. In 1806, the court gave him $50 to repair and clean the new courthouse, and $7 more for rope to do so. He took pride in a contract to keep the city streets clean.

During this time, he bought and sold approximately a dozen slaves, including a woman named Rachel and her child Nancy, who would become an integral part of Timothy's myth. In 1808, he paid $566 for "two-thirds of a negro woman named Joney and her child Hartwell." Later, he acquired another woman named Jane. Surviving records indicate he purchased women and female children, rarely men, and one can suppose from there the work they may have done.

That same year, there was a curious sentence recorded in the Provine papers. It's from a letter, carefully removed from a family bible, written between a Mrs. J. M. Brown and a Mrs. Polk. Timothy's wife Therese, it said, died on November 18, 1808. If this could be verified, it would complicate the theories surrounding Buchanan's Station and the native attack that killed their youngest child, Marie Louise. It would throw an intriguing wrench in the idea that Elizabeth and Timothy got

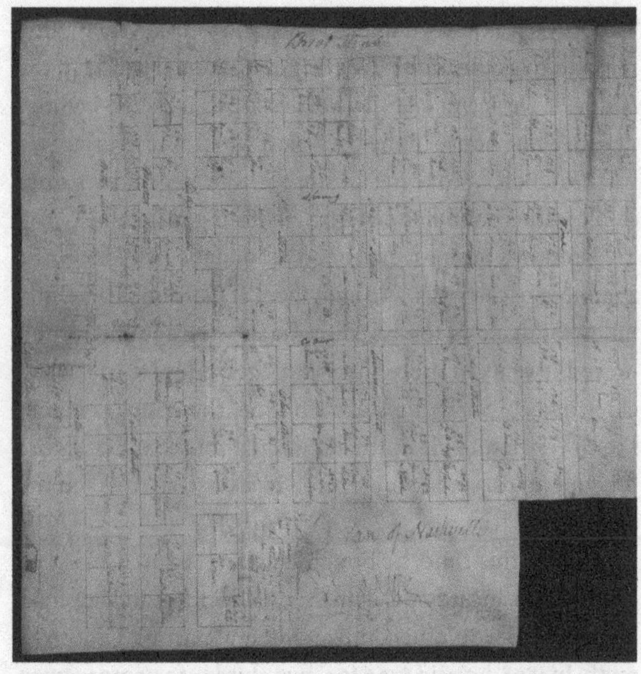

FIGURE 13. The 1805 map of the Plan of Nashville indicates Timothy owned Lot 139 at the time. Image courtesy of Tennessee Historical Society Collection, Tennessee State Library and Archives, Nashville, Tennessee.

back together after Therese disappeared, leaving dozens of new questions unanswered. There are no burial records for Therese in Canada, or at any logical stops along the way—but there are no records in Nashville either. The uncertainty of her final resting spot casts a long shadow over Timothy's burial, which will be addressed later.

Therese now gone, or long gone, Timothy carried on—often surrounded by the most powerful men in town, and likely many of the most beautiful women. As he got older, he never left his home without dressing to the nines in breeches, a

FIGURE 14. "Demonbaum" remains at Lot 139 in this early twentieth-century replica of a Nashville map "made prior to 1800," but likely a replica of the 1805 map. Image courtesy of TSLA Map Collection, Tennessee State Library and Archives, Nashville, Tennessee.

ruffled shirt, and silver buckles, even after the courtly style had faded. He was proudly part Daniel Boone, part Voltaire. These quieter years gave him the opportunity to focus on something that had been so important to his upbringing: Catholicism. After all, he had carefully assured all of his legitimate children were baptized in that faith. (Illegitimate? Too bad).

In 1820, he gathered a group to organize the first Catholic Church in Nashville. For $1, he deeded some of his land, Lot 18, to Arthur Redmond "for and in consideration for the desire to erect a Catholic Church there he can worship the Deity as his fathers did." The next year the first Catholic mass in Nashville was held at Timothy's house; the priest came from nearby Bardstown, Kentucky. Timothy was so moved that he reportedly cried:

> In May of 1821 Bishop Flaget came with Father Abell and were put up with Mr. Montbrun, who received them with tears in his eyes. The first mass in Tennessee was said at the home of Timothy Demonbreun. He was in spiritual desolation from 1771–1821—50 years.

When the Marquis De Lafayette visited Nashville in 1825, Timothy took a seat of honor, and the two spoke happily in French. That now-famous toast to Timothy rang out: "to the grand old man of Tennessee and first white man to settle the Cumberland country." By then, he was no stranger to wine and whiskey—at least according to a nineteenth century *Nashville Banner* article, one supported by court records:

> In his latter days, the old man sat too long with his wine. The unrelenting spirit that made him a fighter and later led him into the unknown wilds of a far country, in these more sedentary days of civilization led him into the depths of the wine jug with the result that he was frequently tipsy and occasionally up for intoxication before the Court of Common Pleas and quarter sessions. But for this general reference to the peccadillos of an unoccupied old age, I find no incident given special mention until very near the end, indeed, the year before his death.

On October 30, 1826, after receiving Catholic rites, Timothy died at his house on Lot 45, now the corner of Third Avenue and Broadway. Though Elizabeth's presence at the house is arguable, who was there when he died was not recorded. He was seventy-nine years old.

A single paragraph in the *Nashville Banner and Nashville Whig* announced his death: "Died, in this town, on Monday evening last, Capt. Timothy Demumbrane, a venerable citizen of Nashville, and the first white man that ever emigrated to this vicinity."

His friend, the silversmith and a future mayor of Nashville, Joseph Elliston, was the executor of his estate.

12

The Trouble with Felix

Timothy's Last Will and Testament

The surviving document is written by Elliston in perfect cursive script, with a steady hand, in measured straight lines, as dictated by Timothy September 24, 1823, five weeks before his death.

> The many days of my existence and my bodily infirmities warn me that I have not long to live. In anticipation of

my departure, I leave the following as my last will and testament . . .

Timothy's wishes unfolded in clear and simple ways. He requested Lot 45 ("on which I now live") be sold as soon as possible. He instructed that the rest be divided between his children in the following manner. To Agnes, five hundred dollars. To Julienne, one thousand dollars and 290 acres of land in Davidson County, where Timothy Jr. was then living. There was one stipulation: it must not interfere with the way Timothy Jr. was using it. Curiously, he gave Timothy Jr. 293 acres of land in Davidson County, including the farm he was living on—plus an equal one thousand dollars. Timothy Jr. by then had married Christina Rains, the daughter of the famous "Indian—and Timothy—fighter" John Rains. This strange split led Julienne, by then married with numerous children of her own, to file a complicated lawsuit in 1833.

Though the will does not mention Elizabeth, Timothy then clearly acknowledged their relationship by leaving his "illigitimate son John B. Demumbrane" five hundred dollars plus a one-third part of a tract of 440 acres outside Nashville. To his "illigitimate daughter . . . Polly Dumumbrane" five hundred dollars and a third of that same land. His very first "illigitimate son William Dumumbrane" also inherited five hundred dollars and the remaining third of the 440 acres.

He also left five hundred dollars to each of his sisters back in Quebec, if they were still alive. His property was sold, including "one old negro woman by the name of Jane" for $100.00 and "sundry pieces of old household and kitchen furniture" for $125.37, to cover debts.

Of all of his still-living children with Therese and Elizabeth, only Felix is left empty-handed. His reasons for leaving Felix out are uncertain, but may have something to do with Felix's rejection of the Catholic Church. Felix had become a Baptist and moved to Kentucky. This religious betrayal theory has holes in it, however, as both John Baptiste and Polly also flirted with the Baptists prior to Timothy's death. Polly was even rebaptized after she married her first cousin, Charles Cagle. They ended up in Illinois with a large family of at least ten children. Timothy Jr. would also convert years later when his wife died and he remarried a Mary Ann Walker. The pair left town for Robertson County. He is buried in Battle Creek Baptist Church Cemetery.

Though there may have been children with other women, including Martha Gray, no other women or children are mentioned in the will. The Demonbreun Society actively seeks out those who may be missing, including the possibility that Timothy could have had children with one of his slaves. The society has one African American member, with the Demonbreun last name from his mother's side.

"We don't know if he had any black children," said current Demonbreun Society president Sue Ellen DeMontbreun Watts. "We would like to know more DNA-wise. Of course, we know he had slaves working around his house. My ancestor Nelly Demonbreun's father used to hear about his relatives buried behind Geist Blacksmith Shop on Jefferson Street. Whether that was a hint that Timothy was buried there, or that Timothy had children buried there, we don't know. Most likely we think they simply took the last name, but we won't know until we get a lot more information in our DNA study.

But if he fathered any children with a black woman then we would like to know, we want to meet the descendants. We have been trying to find them."

Timothy's other known children dispersed across middle Tennessee and Kentucky. William, the "cave baby," ended up with a successful business in the Williamson County, Tennessee, community of Spring Grove despite the fact that he, like all of Timothy's illegitimate children, could not read or write. He claimed to have never known the actual date of his birth. He owned numerous slaves, many of whom at least temporarily used his last name. John Baptiste built a residence "on a commanding eminence in the wildly beautiful hills beyond the confluence of the Little and Big Marrowbone." Many of his fifteen-ish children lived in the valley below, which soon became known as and is still called Demonbreun Valley. The family cemetery, where Elizabeth is buried, and where John Baptiste allegedly but not factually reburied Timothy, is in this valley. It is also rumored, even today, that John Baptiste did not know Timothy was his father until after the War of 1812, when he changed his last name from Derratt to Demonbreun before going into battle.

13

Graverobbers

In what can only be described as a perfect microcosm of Nashville's approach to history, Timothy's final resting place is either lost, moved, or paved over. That's right: nobody knows where he is.

That location is a contentious argument among descendants from each wife. No immediate descendants left any definitive answers to where their father and/or grandfather was buried, leaving everyone—including historians—to argue about this for at least two hundred years. It started remarkably quickly after Timothy's death. In the mid-1800s,

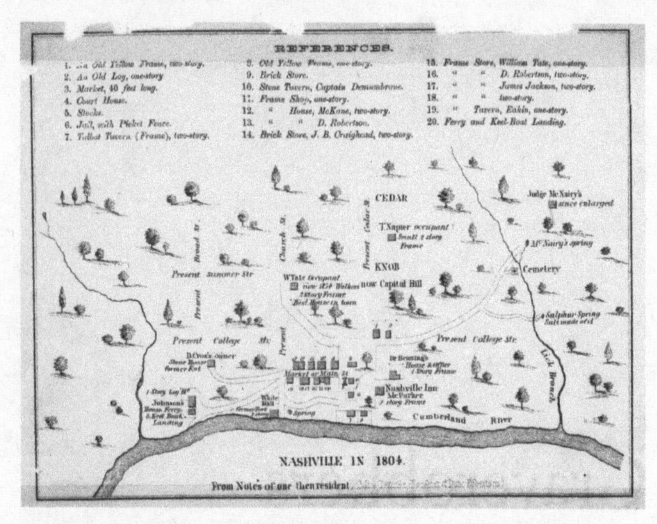

FIGURE 15. An 1804 city map shows the original north-of-town cemetery location near what is now Jefferson Street in the Germantown neighborhood. This map also locates Timothy's "Stone Tavern" on Market Street. Image courtesy of Metro Nashville Archives.

the *Nashville Banner* stated that Timothy was buried in section 28 in the "City Cemetery," but that his remains were moved.

> According to Charles A. Marlin, former superintendent of the City Cemetery, originally Timothy was buried in Section 28 which is the largest section in the cemetery. Mr. Marlin met up with a great grandson who told him that Timothy was buried about 4 miles from Ashland City in Cheatham County.

Since the Union Army destroyed the city's 1822 to 1846 burial records during the Civil War, the chance of any proof is now ash. (Hey, wouldn't Therese's records be around though, if she died in Nashville in 1808? They're not.) It is true Timothy was most likely buried in the original city cemetery, located somewhere between today's First Horizon Park baseball stadium and the Tennessee State Museum along Jefferson Street, possibly between the Third Avenue North and Fourth Avenue North corridor. Early accounts mentioned he was "interred at the little cemetery north of the public square, on a knoll near the sulphur spring where the first settlers had followed herds of buffalo." But was his body moved—and if so, where, and by whom?

Most accounts, including the recent newspaper accounts, placed his body under the parking lot behind what is now Geist restaurant, suspiciously near the cemetery's possible location. Prior to its current iteration as a gastropub, Geist was a blacksmith shop opened in 1886 by German immigrant John Geist Sr. It later served as a lawnmower repair shop.

The Geist location ties into early research conducted by Timothy's great-great grandson H. D. Demonbreun, a former Nashville fire chief. He felt strongly that Timothy was buried in the garden of a "Lot 29" based on oral history from the family. Lot 29 was bounded on the north by Jefferson Street, by Third Avenue to the east, and Fourth Avenue to the west. In June of 1826, it fell into the hands of Nancy Young, the free daughter of two slaves, Will and Rachel, whom Timothy purchased way back in 1787. Nancy may have cared for Timothy in those last few months of his life. Nancy is on record wishing to be buried "in my own garden attached to the dwelling wherein I now live." Lot 29 is now difficult to trace, as it was subdivided and subdivided again into various smaller lots in 1859, the same time many graves were moved from the adjacent cemetery. It is highly possible one of these lots is the one Geist purchased. Though the Young family theory is just that, it's not a wild one. At the time of his death, most of Timothy's children had moved out of the city and, based on the will, there was certainly familial in-fighting. Perhaps in the end it was the Youngs who took care of Timothy's burial arrangements.

The Demonbreun Society's Sue Ellen DeMontbreun Watts also believes Timothy is buried at Geist.

"There were freed slaves who lived on that property," she explained. "One of them took care of Timothy when he was older. They are buried on the back of that property as well. I spoke with the archeological society, we discussed excavating it, but there was too much rubble at the time, and of course now it is paved over. So we may never get definitive answers."

She pointed to a story handed down from her relative Melvin Demonbreun, who, on his way to school at Vanderbilt, would stop at Geist's forge for a rest and a chat. Mr. Geist, it's said, would tell him "son, some of your relatives are buried back here," while pointing out the south window of his shop.

"Some" is of interest because, as we know, a letter stated Therese died in 1808. When Timothy died eighteen years later, that north cemetery was in use. Betsy Phillips posits a logical theory:

> I don't think there's any reason to disbelieve this. There's also some lore that her remains were sent back to Kaskaskia or possibly to Quebec. I think we have plenty of reason to discount this. Moving a body through the wilderness in 1808 either one of those distances would

FIGURE 16. The most likely site of Timothy's grave, now under the parking lot behind Geist Bar and Restaurant in the Germantown neighborhood. Photo by author.

> have been impossible—the smell alone would have been insurmountable. You were buried where you died. If Therese died here, she is buried here. If she died in 1808, she was in that first city cemetery. Though there's compelling circumstantial evidence that he took back up with Elizabeth after her husband died, people in Nashville were buried next to their first spouses. Timothy, I am 99% certain, would have been buried next to Theresa and, since she would have been in the first city cemetery, that's where he would have gone.

If that angle is correct, Therese and Timothy would have been buried side by side in town, in the city cemetery, which might have been adjacent to the home of the freed African American woman who took care of Timothy in his last days.

But another favorite family story complicated that theory by saying that either Elizabeth or John Baptiste exhumed Timothy's body from its resting place and reburied him in the family cemetery far north of town. The motivation is shady but appears rooted in the concept of true love—essentially something along the lines of, "my dad was a total playboy but he loved my mom Elizabeth better than 'aunt' Therese so his body should be out here where she is, not in the city!"—John Baptiste. If Elizabeth was a native, however, she certainly didn't move his body, as that was against tradition. It would not have stopped John Baptiste though, who, again according to legend, drove in a wagon down to Nashville, dug up his father's remains by himself from the Old Cemetery in, accounts say, "SOUTH" Nashville and reburied them in Cheatham County under a simple marker with a small crown on top. South Nashville? Oh no!

Around 1822, Nashville opened up what is now called the City Cemetery, located south of downtown on Fourth Avenue South (as the crow flies, around three miles due south of the O.G. graveyard). This means one of three things: one, he was buried there all along instead—after all it was the newest cemetery at the time of his death, indicating the other likely was either full or had drainage issues; two, he was buried in the north cemetery right before they moved all of the people buried there, including Timothy, to the south cemetery; or, three: they didn't move everybody and he was left by the sulphur springs. In 1986, Louise Davis dug deep—pun intended—into what happened in a feature for the *Tennessean*.

She listed numerous witnesses who claim Timothy's grave was still behind Geist after the cemetery moved.

> The most convincing evidence indicates that Timothy DeMonbreun was never removed from the old North Nashville cemetery where the founding fathers of the city were buried. Even in 1957, when Cate published his article in The Historical Quarterly, he concluded "with considerable conviction," that here was his (DeMonbreun's) natural resting place near the French Lick, on familiar ground and by the side of his earliest pioneer associates.

Davis discovered a very interesting fact, however, in a witness account of the last body exhumed from the north cemetery. In 1859, John Meigs, then twenty-five years old, recalled when his father's body was removed from a "bluff above the sulphur springs." He was so troubled by the state of the cemetery that he drew a number of maps to honor those buried there. Those maps, now owned by the Tennessee Historical Society, show Meigs's father's grave in a bend of Salt Lick Creek, at a spot that lines up perfectly with the location of Geist's blacksmith shop. The original Mr. Geist recalled "a few graves" in an "untouched, narrow strip of the 83-foot-long cemetery" left behind his shop when he opened it thirty years later. He regularly claimed Timothy's grave was one of them. Somewhere between now and then, however, fifteen feet of junk and debris was dumped in the area to prevent flooding, meaning any sort of we-searched-six-to-ten-feet-underground-with-our-penetrating-radar investigation the city or state may have done as new buildings and stadiums were built was completely useless. Timothy would be at least twenty feet below ground today, his rotting remains likely carried away by the now-underground creek to the Cumberland, sending him piece by piece back to the rivers.

14

The Demonbreun Society

In 1975, one of Timothy's descendants, Truman Weldon De Munbrun (you may remember him for his wildly speculative *The Forgotten Frenchman*), started the Demonbreun Society for other family members. The group keeps members up to date on historical resources, manages records, and occasionally takes field trips to visit places important to Timothy's story. The Society keeps an official history, one often updated as more material is discovered, and in 2012, embarked on a DNA project with hopes of answering some of the more challenging Timothy lineage mysteries. Though the project is still in its infancy, it already holds some major clues to the family line.

Heather Ansert, a Kentucky-born descendant of Felix, runs this project for the society. It's built on the work of a Canadian genealogist, Denis Beauregard, who uses triangulation to establish links among Timothy's descendants, and project founder and genealogist Debbie Parker Wayne. Triangulation is a strategy genealogists can use to determine how genetic matches are related. Genetic genealogists create triangles from groups of three autosomal DNA matches to get a better picture of how each member of the group is related to the others. The idea is to resolve inconsistencies in Timothy's paper trail, and to assist members in learning all they can about the complicated family.

The project began with just four male participants that are properly documented descendants, who share the Demonbreun (plus or minus many spellings) surname. This genetic information was analyzed and stored for future comparisons. Then, the project began collecting additional DNA from twelve descendants of Felix and John Baptiste, male and female, to establish the strongest link back to Timothy.

One has to immediately wonder if the DNA was examined for native, versus European, clues. Heather was tight-lipped and careful with her answer.

"The first phase of the TDHS DNA project doesn't contain any specific ethnic information," she said. "Of course all of the DNA information is confidential, but we would like to share some significant aspects of the DNA project's findings with interested parties in the future. It is anticipated that additional DNA donors to this first phase will allow for a discussion about the descendants and ancestors' ethnicity."

So is there anything that helps us unravel the Elizabeth versus Therese mystery?

"A very notable aspect of the DNA project's first phase is that female donors were eager to trace their lineage to Elizabeth and Therese," she explained.

But the line of questioning ends there, with a caveat.

"In 2012, Glenda Merhoff, a now-deceased descendant and former DNA project chairperson, commissioned a report on Felix," she added. "Although the DNA wasn't a contributing factor to any of the report's conclusions, its documentation 'strongly supports' a conclusion that Felix is a 'natural son of Timothy Demonbreun and Elizabeth Bennett.'"

This could change everything—and potentially explain why Felix is left out of Timothy's will. But it's far too early to start down that route, which, if true, could change the story significantly.

The Felix report is not available to the public at this time. And there's much work to do on the DNA; in fact, there are hopes that the Society can work more directly with Beauregard on the triangulation aspect, as well as dig into more details of each participant's genetic code.

Two massive questions remain; each likely could be answered in time by this project. Can we rule in or rule out Elizabeth being a Native American? And, what about African Americans with the last name Demonbreun or variations thereof? Their stories are barely told.

The DNA project is a bigger, more scientific extension of the Society's large genealogy database. That database, run by member Dick Staley, has more than twenty-eight thousand documented descendants. It's a database that grows weekly, Dick explained, as certain members dig in deeper to connect the dots. There are weeks where he verifies and adds more than a hundred new family members to Timothy's tree.

Today, Sue Ellen DeMontbreun Watts leads the one hundred members of the society. She is sad that the membership is far down from its peak of more than one thousand decades ago. She spells her name in one of numerous iterations of the original. It's all because of one of John Baptiste's grandsons, who studied medicine at Vanderbilt University in the 1880s. There, a teacher told him he was spelling his last name wrong, that it should be "DeMontbreun," so to make his professor happy, he made the change. His cousins, Sue Ellen's direct line, made the change as well. Her legacy as a DeMontbreun was a big part of her experience growing up in Nashville.

"My grandmother, Varna Mavis DeMontbreun, died from the Spanish flu when my father was a month old," she recalled. "His father, Lurton, moved everyone out of town a little toward Madison to regroup, before coming back to a little house in Inglewood, in East Nashville. And that's where I was born in 1943. My father and his brother joined up to fight the world war, so my aunts took care of me. One of them was Mattie DeMontbreun, charter member of the French Lick Branch of the Daughters of the American Revolution (DAR). She was a huge historian.

"On Saturdays, Mattie would take me to get a BBQ sandwich and take rides around Spring Hill cemetery. We'd sit on tombstones, eat sandwiches, and drink our orange drink. I was there when she had DAR meetings at her house. I'd stand up and say the pledge of allegiance the first time they added 'one nation under God' to it. I can still see her sitting there proud as a peacock. She died when I was twelve, and it was one of the most devastating deaths I've suffered. She ruled the house. I knew about Timothy as long as I could remember, because of her."

When she was a kid, Sue Ellen heard a lot of stories about Timothy from Mattie and other family members. She says she remembers the basics: he was a French fur trader, one of the first white men in Nashville. She was told her last name was an old Nashville name, one she should be very proud of. She heard there was a cave, but didn't see it until she took a boat tour down the Cumberland River, before the cave's entrance was blocked by wire and fencing. She admits members of the Society have since crawled through the fence to get in and explore.

"It's really rough in there now," she added.

Sue Ellen worries about some recent retellings of Timothy's story, particularly accounts that make Timothy sound illiterate.

"I think he should be portrayed not only for what he did in Nashville but everything else he did. I know in depth where he came from and his family history in Canada, and his great-grandfather Pierre," she said. "He came from a highly educated group. That part really fascinated me about him. It's not just Timothy the frontier man, it was Timothy Demonbreun and all the other things he had. I'm fascinated by why he left Canada as the British came, and wonder what happened in Kaskaskia, and I can't imagine traveling from Quebec to here with no roads and no cars."

She feels confident he left Canada because the British took over, but Kaskaskia remains more of a mystery.

> I've been there, and of course the geography shifted so much after the earthquake that you can't really see and understand what it must have been like. It made me think of Therese, when and why she came to Nashville. And why does she disappear from the record after the last child's baptism the way she does? Some Society members think she never came to Nashville. But I wonder, when there was the big Indian attack at Mansker's Station, well, Timothy had already built his house downtown then, and it was big [sources note it has a large stable for twenty horses, etc. and it was referred to as a "commodious dwelling"]. He gave that house to Elizabeth and Joseph. Why did he do that? That's what I want to know? Well, I think he was getting ready to bring his family to Nashville. He was back in Kaskaskia for that last baptism, but I don't think Therese died during that time, Kaskaskia has great records, so we would have seen that.

This timeline, and Timothy's adulterous or nonadulterous intent, is one of the most hotly debated issues in the Society. The members also argue about where Timothy is buried, one of the many facts versus assumptions they hope to dispel with evidence.

"A lot of Timothy's life makes for a very good story," Sue Ellen said. "Some things are true, and some we simply do not know. He remains a mystery because we have a lot of information but we haven't met him personally. If we talked to him we'd have a lot of answers, and a lot of questions. But right now all we have is words and feelings.

"We all wonder what happened in those years Therese was gone," added Connie Thomas, the society's vice president. "And was Elizabeth an Indian? I've heard Elizabeth was called an Indian because she lived like an Indian. There's been much discussion around here on Elizabeth over the past decade, though, but not much on Therese. So I really wonder about her."

Connie is descended from John Baptiste, the mostly confirmed illegitimate son. She claims she has the "Demonbreun nose: the largest nose you've ever seen", and that her grandfather had it as well. Born at Baptist Hospital (now Saint Thomas) in Nashville, she became obsessed with her heritage after an uncle gave her a copy of *The Forgotten Frenchmen*. Growing up along Marrowbone Creek, she also heard numerous family tales that Timothy was the "father of Nashville" and that Elizabeth was an Indian, which made her believe she, too, must be part Cherokee (hey, DNA project?). Today, she owns a Demonbreun quilt embroidered with dozens of the family members' names, and a horn she believes is from John Baptiste. She used to wander the land where the two creeks merge, looking for remnants of his cabin.

Her life along Marrowbone Creek, of course, was a result of John Baptiste's choice to leave Nashville for the countryside.

Sue Ellen and Connie both wonder about the truth behind Timothy's complex romantic relationships.

"I think Timothy was a man who was gone a long time," Sue Ellen laughed. "And he needed a woman, and I think Elizabeth was available. I don't know much about her personality but it seems she was what you would call streetwise now, so wilderness-wise. And having her around was a good thing."

"Elizabeth seems like she's very strong," Connie added. "She had so many hardships, but ended up living so long. I have heard there were some other ladies, but I don't know. Overall, it seemed like a rough life for Timothy. I'd hate to be Therese knowing he had a common-law wife in Nashville. My understanding is he tried to marry Elizabeth but she wasn't Catholic, so they wouldn't condone it. The reason he took on this other wife is that Therese disappeared all those years. Did he think she was dead? I often try to justify him having two wives. People did things in the moment according to their surroundings, and that's likely why he acted that way."

Both women agree, however, that the Society's main concern is Timothy's legacy, and how to tell his many stories as a whole, how to move beyond the caricature of the man who lived in a cave and might have founded Nashville—how to separate the myth and the history in a way that fairly, and authentically, honors his contributions.

"We have the statue," Connie said, "but I feel like you simply don't hear much about Timothy anymore. When I visit New Orleans, they know his family. New Orleans and Canada have that connection, and I think Nashville should be aware of ours. I'd love to see March 23 be Timothy Demonbreun day, but Nashville doesn't acknowledge it. It's an educational opportunity lost."

The statue she references is the sort of strong-man-cum-adventurer bronze one expects as a natural extension of the

FIGURE 17. The Alan LeQuire statue of Timothy tops the Cumberland River bluffs along Nashville's riverfront. Photo by author.

FIGURE 18. Timothy's descendants supported the statue's creation by purchasing engraved bricks. Photo by author.

myth. Created in 1996 and funded jointly by the Society and the state, it stands along the west bank of the Cumberland River, adjacent to the recreated Fort Nashborough, spitting distance from the busy party district on Lower Broadway. In fact, it's no stretch to say that bachelorettes on pedal taverns regularly scream-sing the lyrics of "Family Tradition" or "I've Got Friends in Low Places" at Timothy's likeness. Sculpted by Alan LeQuire, the creator of *Musica* (which sits somewhat ironically at the top of Demonbreun Street at the entrance to Music Row) and the monumental *Athena Parthenos* across town at Nashville's replica of the Parthenon, the work has been praised as "heroic" and "handsome."

Sue Ellen hopes he is remembered for so much more than the Paul Bunyan-in-bronze the city chose.

"He had a good education, good spiritual background, he was adventurous and he cared for his children," Sue Ellen said. "I don't know how he felt about his wife, but he did take care of all his children, legit and non-legit. Some people you can describe in a few words, but he is an extremely varied person. He had many interests such as fur trapping and exporting, he was a leader as governor of a territory; he must have had a good sharp mind. All of that combined with his family history and sense of adventure, I think he would have been a very interesting person to sit down and talk to and have deep conversations. I see him as being so many, many different things.

"We have the street, and sure we have that statue, but most people have no idea who he is or what is really involved here. The fur trading and the cave are exciting but that misses the whole picture. In fact, when I think of the name of the city being changed from Nashborough to Nashville, the English version versus the French version, I bet he was a huge influence on the name of the city and a big part of why we call it that today."

15

The Gun, the Watch, and the Desk

Timothy left many things behind when he died that October day at Lot 45. There was a lot of land and some furniture. There were also enslaved humans, and varying amounts of cash to legitimate and illegitimate children alike (sorry again, Felix). Even though there was a relatively clear last will and testament, Timothy's complex life left a divided group of heirs to argue, exploit, and/or honor the many questions and myths of his complicated story. Each child had numerous children, creating army after army to defend each side of the truth.

But what became of his tangible belongings? What can we still hold in our hands today to connect with him? Three items come up frequently: the gun, the watch, and the desk. The whereabouts of each are a veritable Holy Grail–style mystery, with no treasure map left behind, only a handful of clues and mentions as two of the items faded into the unknown by the turn of the twentieth century, while one possibly became a famous piece of American furniture.

In 1858, a German immigrant named E. L. Faller came to Nashville and set up a watch repair shop on Deaderick Street. For years, businessmen and the wealthy would browse his shop for the best in antique time machines, or drop by when their watch needed a spring nudged, a bezel replaced, or a dial polished. There, in the dust and ticking, perhaps hanging on the wall or laid beneath glass beside others that had kept time for so many years, was a watch allegedly owned by Timothy. E. L., however, was not long for America, as he killed himself in a "brains scattered on every side" (thank you, *Nashville Republican Banner*), self-inflicted hunting accident at Cockrill's Bend just twenty-one years later. He left the business to his son, L. A.

When L. A. moved the business a few blocks over, to the upper floor of the Arcade, and hung his painted sign, "L. A. Faller's, Watchmaker," was Timothy's watch with him? The trail ends with the Fallers.

According to the Demonbreun Society, the locations of the watch and Timothy's gun are currently unknown. The gun is a shotgun, a flintlock, brought from Quebec, perhaps itself a veteran of the Battle of the Plains of Abraham, where it may have been steadily held to Timothy's father's shoulder as he fired at the advancing English.

In 1878, writing about Timothy, Judge Jo C. Guild said that one of Timothy's grandsons, William R. DeMonbreun ("a most estimable citizen"), had the gun. At a meeting of the Tennessee Historical Society on March 24, 1880, members discussed the fact that a Mrs. Felix Abbey would loan the watch and gun to the group for display at the city's first Centennial celebration. It was indeed seen there in 1880. But then it is never heard about again. Historians have searched for the watch and the gun at length. In the 1930s, writer Kathryn De Monbreun Whitefort made "every effort" to locate the gun and watch, including writing to many possible owners, but came up empty-handed.

The desk, however, is another case all together. A man named John Gordon, a.k.a. "Captain of the Spies" for his behavior during the American Revolution, moved west from Virginia to Nashville at the end of that conflict. His reputation as an Indian fighter led territorial governor William Blount to give him a commission as a captain in the mounted infantry, and when Tennessee was granted statehood, he was appointed postmaster of Nashville. It was perhaps due to that position that he acquired the desk. It's a desk of epic proportions, nearly nine feet tall and made of solid black walnut. With numerous drawers and secret compartments, it was a perfect place to manage more than just the mail. And the story—not fully verified—goes that John got it from Timothy. John also went on to do a bunch of damage in the Creek Wars, and perhaps let his friend Andrew Jackson write a letter or two at that desk. This desk remains in the Gordon family, handed down through six generations. Recent family research indicates it was made in Danville, Virginia, around 1760.

Hints of many of Demonbreun's belongings' whereabouts echoed across the 1800s, with deafening silence for most settling in by the early 1900s. The Demonbreun name, however, lived on downtown for quite a while, with a saloon owned by Timothy's great-grandson, Bynum R. Demonbreun. The Demonbreun saloon was located on the Public Square from at least 1889 to 1910. Bynum lived above the saloon, and created tokens as a way to encourage patrons to spend more than their worth. As one of more than 156 saloons listed downtown in 1899, advertising was certainly required. His saloon went the way of Prohibition, and was later razed in the urban renewal destruction of most of the public square in the early 1970s. One has to wonder if the gun or the watch might have found its way to Bynum, and might have been sitting quietly above the noise of a drunk crowd, boxed up and taken away when alcohol went underground.

Like the gun, the watch, and the desk, so many parts of Timothy's story are still out there, whereabouts unknown. This book was written across 2020, a year when the pandemic prevented safe travel for further research in Vincennes, Indiana, or to the Illinois State Archives to deep-dive the

Kaskaskia records—and, perhaps even more importantly, to Quebec to research birth, baptism, and marriage records. There is still work left to be done, to tighten up the timeline of Timothy's travels between Kaskaskia and Nashville, to clarify his relationship with women other than Therese and Elizabeth, to connect the dots on other children he may have fathered, and to understand his romantic choices. The Demonbreun Society's DNA project is likely to reveal what we have right and what we have very wrong. And though it may never be solved, the mystery of his final resting place remains a perfect metaphor for his influence on Nashville's early years. His genius may lie in that disappearing trick alone, a man who could fly under the radar, befriend natives and various Europeans with ease. He was at home on a canoe on the Wabash or dressed in fine silks sharing whiskey with the Marquis de Lafayette. He was clearly charming; women were drawn to him for safety, comfort, and conversation. He wrote like a novelist and likely moved through society like a true chameleon, protecting his and his family's interests above all else. He could dissuade generals with a simple letter, charm them with conversation, end a fight with a gregarious right hook or a clever turn of phrase, or win the trust of a lover or friend despite his duplicitous actions. His influence was immense, though his body, like the truth in some of his most fascinating stories, has disappeared somewhere beneath the city of Nashville.

NOTES

CHAPTER 1

8 "spindly but strong legs." Truman Weldon De Munbrun, *The Forgotten Frenchman: The Public and Private Life of Jacques Timothe Boucher Sieur de Montbrun* (Nashville, TN: Jacques Timothe Boucher Sieur de Montbrun Heritage Society, 1977).

9 "the grand old man of Tennessee." Josephus Conn Guild, *Old Times in Tennessee* (Nashville, TN: Tavel, Eastman and Howell, 1878).

CHAPTER 2

13 "seventy yards off the river." Demonbreun Society Online Archives.

16 "Of course the *Nashville American*." *Nashville Daily American*, February 11, 1879, 4.

22 "Were present Mr. Thimothe Boucher." Yves Drolet, *Dictionnaire Généalogique et Héraldique de la Noblesse Canadienne Française du XVII au XIX Siècle* (Montreal: Dico, 2010).

23 "And as the parties wish to give." Drolet, *Dictionnaire Généalogique.*

CHAPTER 5

37 "more traditional housing 'in town.'" Demonbreun Society Online Archives.

CHAPTER 6

42 "He behaved himself as a friend." Demonbreun Society Online Archives.
44 "best wishes for his successor." Demonbreun Society Online Archives.
44 "There's an 1848 newspaper article." Demonbreun Society Online Archives.

CHAPTER 8

56 "Between Timothy Demunbre of Davidson County." Land Deeds folder, Demonbreun Society Online Archives.

CHAPTER 9

63 "To all Home It May Consarn." John Montgomery, letter to General Clark to the services rendered by Jacques Timothe de Montbrun to the Americans, October 17, 1780. Demonbreun Society Online Archives.
64 "The good understanding." Demonbreun Society Online Archives.

CHAPTER 10

68 "Many years past I happened." Tennessee governor John Sevier, letter to Major Amos Stoddard, October 9, 1810. Demonbreun Society Online Archives.
69 "Sometime in August preceding." Sevier, letter to Major Amos Stoddard.

CHAPTER 11

74 "It appears that DeMonbreun." Demonbreun Society Online Archives.
75 "An 1811 rental listing." *Nashville Democrat Clarion and Tennessee Gazette*, February 1, 1811.
77 "For $1, he deeded some of his land." Demonbreun Society Online Archives.
78 "That now-famous toast." Guild, *Old Times in Tennessee*.

CHAPTER 12

81 "The many days of my existence." Will of Timothy Demonbreun as transcribed by Joseph Elliston, September 24, 1823. Demonbreun Society Online Archives.
84 "on a commanding eminence." Demonbreun Society Online Archives.

CHAPTER 13

87 "in my own garden." Bruce Barlar et al. "A Critique of the Timothy Demonbreun and Sulfur Dell Research Project" (Murfreesboro, TN: A Public Service Project of the Historic Preservation Program and the Center for Historic Preservation at Middle Tennessee State University, 1986).

CHAPTER 15

106 "brains scattered on every side." *Nashville Republican Banner*, November 4, 1871, 4.

BIBLIOGRAPHY

Adams, George Rollie, and Ralph Jerry Christian. *Nashville: A Pictorial History* (Norfolk, Virginia: The Donning Company, 1988), 6–8.

Ansert, Heather. Interview with the author, Nashville, TN, October 8, 2020.

Arnow, Harriette Simpson. *Flowering of the Cumberland* (Lincoln, NE: Bison Books, 1963).

———. *Seedtime on the Cumberland* (Lincoln, NE: Bison Books, 1960).

Barlar, Bruce, Bonnie Gamble, Sandra Glidden, Blossom Merryman, and Ben Nance. "A Critique of the Timothy Demonbreun and Sulfur Dell Research Project" (Murfreesboro, TN: A Public Service Project of the Historic Preservation Program and the Center for Historic Preservation at Middle Tennessee State University, 1986).

Belting, Natalia Maree. *Kaskaskia under the French Regime* (Carbondale: Southern Illinois University Press, 1948).

Brown, Margaret K. *The Voyageur in the Illinois Country: The Fur Trade's Professional Boatman in Mid America* (St. Louis, MO: Center for French Colonial Studies, 2002).

Bucy, Carole. Interview with the author, Nashville, September 28, 2020.

Burt, Jesse C. *Nashville Its Life and Times* (Nashville: Tennessee Book Company, 1959).

Cate, Wirt Armistead. "Timothy Demonbreun," *Tennessee Historical Quarterly* 16, no. 3 (September 1957).

Davis, Louise. "DeMonbreun Burial Spot Still a Mystery," *Tennessean*, January 5, 1986.

———. "Mysterious DeMonbreun Comes into Clear Focus," *Tennessean*, May 19, 1985.

De Munbrun, Truman Weldon. *The Forgotten Frenchman: The Public and Private Life of Jacques Timothe Boucher Sieur de Montbrun* (Nashville, TN: Jacques Timothe Boucher Sieur de Montbrun Heritage Society, 1977).

Demonbreun, David Henry, and James Edward Demonbreun. *Family Ledger* (Nashville: Tennessee State Library and Archives, 1860–1902).

Demonbreun Society Online Archives, with permission from Dick D. Staley, accessed July through December, 2020. The Demonbreun Society archives are privately held and accessible with permission from the Society.

Drake, Doug, Jack Masters, and Bill Puryear. *Founding of the Cumberland Settlements*, vol. 1 (Gallatin, TN: Warioto Press, 2009).

Drolet, Yves. *Dictionnaire Généalogique et Héraldique de la Noblesse Canadienne Française du XVII au XIX Siècle* (Montreal: Dico, 2010).

Ely, James W. "Andrew Jackson as Tennessee State Court Judge, 1798–1804," *Tennessee Historical Quarterly* 40, no. 2 (Summer 1981).

———. "The Legal Practice of Andrew Jackson," *Tennessee Historical Quarterly* 38, no. 4 (Winter 1979).

Gordon, John Steele. "The Other John Gordon," *American Heritage*, Volume 48, Issue 33, May/June 1997.

Guild, Josephus Conn. *Old Times in Tennessee*. (Nashville, TN: Tavel, Eastman and Howell, 1878).

James, James Alton. *George Rogers Clark Papers 1771–1781* (Springfield: Illinois State Historical Library, 1912).

"Limothe De Montebreune: A Romantic Chapter in Our Local History," *Memphis Public Ledger*, February 13, 1879.

MacDonald, David, and Raine Waters. *Kaskaskia: The Lost Capitol of Illinois* (Carbondale: Southern Illinois University Press, 2019).

Nash, Robert T. "From Germantown and Valley Forge to Middle Tennessee: A Research Note on Land Grants and Paying for the North Carolina Continental Line," *Tennessee Historical Quarterly* 73, no. 4 (Winter 2014).

Phillips, Betsy. "In Search of Granny 'Rat's Tavern," *Nashville Scene*, October 27, 2009.

———. "Where's Elizabeth Durard's Statue?," *Nashville Scene*, August 17, 2009.

Provine, William. *Jacques Timothe the Voucher: Genealogical and Biographical Data* folder (Nashville: Tennessee State Library and Archives).

———. *Joseph Deraque* folder (Nashville: Tennessee State Library and Archives).

Simmons, Bunny. *Timothy Demonbreun, The Noble Frontiersman*, http://www.timothydemonbreun.com/Timothys_Story.html (accessed October 2020).

Staley, Dick. Interview with the author via e-mail, July–October 2020.

Summerville, James. *Southern Epic: Nashville through Two Hundred Years* (Gloucester Point, VA: Hallmark Publishing, 1996) 15, 22–23.

Thomas, Connie. Interview with the author, Nashville, September 24, 2020.

"Two Centuries of Nashville," *Tennessean*, April 28, 1909.

Walker, Hugh. *Tennessee Tales* (Nashville, TN: Aurora Publishers, 1970), 170.

Watts, Sue Ellen DeMontbreun. Interview with the author, Nashville, September 14, 2020.

Whitefort, Kathryn De Monbreun. *A Genealogy and History of Jacques Timothe Boucher Sieur De Monbreun and His Ancestors and Descendants* (Ann Arbor, MI: Edwards Brothers, 1939).

Wills, Ridley. *Nashville Streets and Their Stories* (Franklin, TN: Plumbline Media, 2012), 39.

Zepp, George R. "Demonbreun Saloon Location Cleared in '70s Urban Renewal," *Tennessean*, May 10, 2006.

———. *Hidden History of Nashville* (Charleston, SC: History Press, 2009), 17–18.

Zibart, Carl F. *Yesterday's Nashville* (Miami, FL: E. A. Seemann Publishing, 1976), 12–13.

CPSIA information can be obtained
at www.ICGtesting.com
Printed in the USA
LVHW041526250222
712023LV00021B/2663